高等学校翻译专业本科教材

总主编：仲伟合　何刚强

应用翻译教程

APPLIED TRANSLATION

彭萍　编著

外语教学与研究出版社
FOREIGN LANGUAGE TEACHING AND RESEARCH PRESS
北京 BEIJING

图书在版编目（CIP）数据

应用翻译教程 / 彭萍编著. -- 北京 ：外语教学与研究出版社，2023.5
高等学校翻译专业本科教材 / 仲伟合，何刚强总主编
ISBN 978-7-5213-4553-7

Ⅰ. ①应… Ⅱ. ①彭… Ⅲ. ①英语－翻译－高等学校－教材 Ⅳ. ①H315.9

中国国家版本馆 CIP 数据核字（2023）第 107865 号

出 版 人　王　芳
责任编辑　屈海燕
责任校对　曹　妮
封面设计　覃一彪　水长流文化
版式设计　付玉梅
出版发行　外语教学与研究出版社
社　　址　北京市西三环北路 19 号（100089）
网　　址　https://www.fltrp.com
印　　刷　三河市北燕印装有限公司
开　　本　787×1092　1/16
印　　张　12.5
版　　次　2023 年 8 月第 1 版　2023 年 8 月第 1 次印刷
书　　号　ISBN 978-7-5213-4553-7
定　　价　45.90 元

如有图书采购需求，图书内容或印刷装订等问题，侵权、盗版书籍等线索，请拨打以下电话或关注官方服务号：
客服电话：400 898 7008
官方服务号：微信搜索并关注公众号“外研社官方服务号”
外研社购书网址：https://fltrp.tmall.com

物料号：345530001

目　录

编者的话

应用翻译在翻译实践中最常见。在经济飞速发展、科学技术突飞猛进的今天，社会各单位对应用翻译的需求大幅上升，特别是在经贸、旅游、科技、法律以及国际事务等方面。有鉴于此，本教材选取常用的十种实用类文体进行讲解，希望能够帮助翻译学习者掌握相关文体的文体特点、翻译策略和翻译原则。这十种文体分别是机构介绍、产品介绍与说明、广告宣传、商务期刊、旅游、科技、法律、礼仪文书、政府与组织文件、新闻。笔者从事翻译工作二十余年，除中国文化、哲学和历史外，这十类也是翻译时经常遇到的文体。

本教材按上述文体分为十个单元，每个单元由四个模块组成，以下是每个模块的内容介绍。

第一模块为翻译概述。该模块首先对相关文体及其翻译进行简单界定和综述。接着分别介绍英文和中文相关文体的语篇特点，并针对提到的特点举例说明翻译的技巧和策略。讲解涉及用词特点以及句式特点，有些文体会涉及修辞特点。该部分力求文体特点归纳到位、讲解细致、举例翔实。最后会根据前面的讲解归纳相关文体的翻译原则，并列表归纳所讲解的文体特点及相应翻译策略。

第二模块为语篇汉译解析。该模块选择250词左右的相关文体英文语篇，对其中涉及的文体特点和其他语言特点及其翻译策略进行详细讲解和分析，最后给出参考译文。

第三模块为语篇英译解析。该模块选取350字左右的相关文体中文语篇，对其中涉及的文体特点和其他语言特点及其翻译策略进行详细讲解和分析，最后给出参考译文。

第四模块为翻译练习。翻译工作者一般从事的都是语篇翻译，因此本模块选取相应文体的语篇作为翻译练习，包括一篇英译中和一篇中译英，英文语篇单词数在100—200之间，中文语篇字数在200—250之间。希望学习者通过该模块温习和巩固相应的学习成果。

本教材为英汉双向翻译教材，旨在使读者学习同一文体翻译时能够做到英汉语互相比较、对照。通过每一文体的英文语篇和中文语篇的学习和翻译，读者能够更好地发现英汉两种语言的差别所在，从而让自己的译文更加地道，更彰显目的语文本的特点。此外，希望学习者通过学习相关应用文体的翻译，以后不仅能够从事相关翻译工作，更能用中文或英文直接撰写相应的文章。特别需要指出的是，为体现翻译教材与时俱进的特点，本教材选用的译例和练习材料均为编写时所能找到的最新材料。

本教材虽为应用翻译教材，实际上对提高综合翻译能力也有一定帮助。因此，本教材不仅适合作为本科生和翻译硕士相应课程的翻译教材，也适合广大翻译学习者学习翻译时使用。另外，本书提供的讲解部分和练习部分的所有参考译文绝非完美，因为翻译是一个不断打磨和完善的过程，任何译文均和写文章一样“不厌百回改”，在保证意思传达正确、表达正确的前提下，不同译者的译文均会有所不同。希望读者客观地看待这些译文，在参考所有译文的基础上能够给出更完美的翻译，那也正是编者的心愿。

感谢外语教学与研究出版社编辑为本书出版付出的辛勤劳动，感谢我的2021级翻译硕士生刘雨霏、罗哲安、罗怡昕、陈佳彬、仲诗佳、吴文卓和郑依婷帮助校对书稿，感谢我的先生刘辛利用业余时间对书稿格式进行了检查并排版。需要说明的是，本教材在编写过程中参考了诸多资料，在此一并表示感谢。

彭萍

2021年冬于平心斋

第一单元　机构介绍

第一模块：机构介绍翻译概述

机构介绍，顾名思义，就是指各种组织机构的介绍性和宣传性文字，比如公司简介和宣传、学校简介和社会组织简介等，主要介绍其工作性质、组织构成、历史沿革、业务范围、市场前景、服务或经营理念以及其他有关情况，从而使得公众对其有一定的了解，以树立机构的形象、达到宣传效果。中英文的机构介绍文字一般都比较简单，但会使用一些说明性、推介性、宣传性的词汇，从而帮助实现介绍和宣传的目的。当然，由于中英文背后的思维模式存在差异，两种语言中的机构介绍在用词和句式结构方面依然存在一些不同。所以，下文分别讲解英文机构介绍和中文机构介绍的文体特点及其翻译。

一、英文机构介绍文体特点及其翻译

（一）用词特点

首先，英文的机构介绍材料在介绍相关信息时往往使用较为简单的词汇，浅显易懂，照顾到各个层次的读者。翻译时，也尽量选用一些普通词汇，但由于中文介绍材料有时描述性相对较强，所以译文在措辞上也要增加一点美感。请看下面的例子：

例1

The International Association of Prosecutors (IAP) is the only worldwide organization of prosecutors. It was established in 1995 and now has more than 180 organizational members from over 177 different countries and regions,

representing every continent, as well as many individual members.
国际检察官协会是全球唯一的国际性检察官组织。协会成立于1995年，目前拥有来自五大洲、超过177个国家和地区的180多个团体会员以及众多个人会员。

例2

Nestled high above Lake Geneva with an outstanding view on the lake and close to Geneva International Airport, Nescens Clinique de Genolier is specialized in preventive health, lifestyle diseases management, and anti-aging.
吉尼列尔妮尚希诊所位于日内瓦国际机场附近，坐落在日内瓦湖上方，可以眺望美丽的湖景。诊所主要提供预防保健、生活习惯病治疗和抗衰老方面的医疗服务。

例3

Naturally, PostBus Switzerland is not only concerned with groups but also about the individual traveler who would like to explore Switzerland under their own steam.
当然，瑞士邮政巴士不仅为团体游客提供服务，还为喜欢独自探索瑞士的散客提供各种帮助。

以上三个例子分别是协会、诊所和巴士的介绍，旨在提供信息，所以原文大多数词汇都相对简单，翻译起来不算困难，但是汉语译文要注意措辞正式，有些地方在审美方面还要注意照顾到中国读者的预期。

由于机构介绍涉及机构的工作性质或专业领域，所以这类文体中会出现一些专业术语，翻译时也要在汉语中找到对应的表述，像上面例1中的prosecutor，例2中的preventive health，lifestyle diseases management和anti-aging，例3中的individual traveler等。再看下面一个例子：

例4

Working with 194 Member States, across six regions, and from more than 150 offices, WHO staff is united in a shared commitment to achieve better health for everyone, everywhere. Together we strive to combat diseases—communicable diseases like influenza and HIV, and non-communicable diseases like cancer and heart disease.
世界卫生组织共有六个区域，194个成员国，其工作人员在150多个办事处开展工作，共同致力于增进世界各地每一个人的健康。我们一起努力防治疾病，包括流感和艾滋病毒等传染病以及癌症和心脏病等非传染性疾病。

该段选自世界卫生组织（WHO）的介绍，里面有一些表述比较专业，如Member States 要译成"成员国"，communicable diseases 要译成"传染病"，influenza 要译成"流感"，HIV要译成"艾滋病毒"等。

（二）句式特点

英语机构介绍文本的句子一般不会太长，因为既然是介绍类的文字，就需要照顾到最广大的读者，使广大读者没有什么阅读障碍就理解原文的意思，把握原文的信息。同时，介绍类文本很多时候也是一种宣传，如果句子太长就起不到宣传的作用。翻译时需要注意中文的衔接与连贯，可使用一些小分句。

例5

The Food and Agriculture Organization (FAO) is a specialized agency of the United Nations that leads international efforts to defeat hunger. Our goal is to achieve food security for all and make sure that people have regular access to enough high-quality food to lead active, healthy lives. With 195 members—194 countries and the European Union, FAO works in over 130 countries worldwide. We believe that everyone can play a part in ending hunger.

联合国粮农组织（FAO）是联合国专业机构，致力于带领全球消除饥饿，实现全人类粮食安全，并保证人们定期获得充足的优质食物，从而积极健康地生活。联合国粮农组织目前拥有195名成员，包括194个成员国和欧洲联盟，在全球130多个国家开展工作，相信人人都可以为消除饥饿作出自己的贡献。

该段是联合国粮农组织的简介，一共四句话，虽然有三句都是复合句，但不是特别复杂。第三句是简单句，翻译时可以与第四句合并。

例6

We've always believed in serving the finest coffee possible. It's our goal for all our coffee to be grown under the highest standards of quality. Our coffee buyers personally travel to coffee farms in Latin America, Africa, and Asia to select high-quality Arabica beans.

我们一直致力于尽可能提供最优质的咖啡，旨在保证所有咖啡均符合最高质量标准。我们的咖啡采购人员足迹遍布拉丁美洲、非洲和亚洲，旨在选择最优质的阿拉比卡咖啡豆。

该段是咖啡馆简介，三句话都是简单句，其中第二句和第三句较长，里面含一些短语。翻译时可以将短语译为汉语的小分句。

二、中文机构介绍文体特点及其翻译

（一）用词特点

中文机构介绍用词一般比较正式，而且尽可能使用富有感染力的词汇，尤其是四字成语，以实现介绍和宣传的目的。翻译时可根据情况，在保持原文信息和美感的前提下，将译文适当简单化，因为前文讲过，英文的介绍宣传材料不会过多使用复杂的词汇。

例7

国际组织学院是集教学科研、人才培养、智库研究、人才推送为一体的教学研究型机构。

The School of International Organizations is a teaching and research institution oriented for talent cultivation and production and think tank research.

例8

我公司是全球性的印钞造币衍生品供应商，全面负责总公司的市场开发工作。

We are a global supplier of banknote printing and minting derivatives, engaged in market development for our parent company.

例9

我公司汇集了大学的特殊优势和20年的市场积累，以品牌、资源、资金为发展支点，以“简单、高效、健康”为管理思想，突出主营业务方向，并依此架构了三个业务群组：自有品牌产品群组、自有技术应用群组和渠道增值分销群组。公司力求以多样化的产品、系统化的技术应用和服务，多层次、持续性地满足消费者和用户的需求。

With strong support from the university and 20 years of business experience, our company, based on its brand name, resources and capital, and its philosophy of simplicity, efficiency and health, has established three business sectors, namely, production, technology application, and distribution. Its ultimate goal is to satisfy the needs of customers with diverse products and systematic technical applications and services.

以上三个例子分别是学院和企业的介绍，措辞均比较正式，译文根据前面提到的英文机构介绍类文本用词特点进行了一定的简化处理。有些机构的中文宣传材料充满渲染语气的描述性词汇，也需要简化处理，请看下面的例子：

例10

饭店集中国传统神韵与西方现代风格于一体，庄重、富丽、典雅。大堂的八根镀金大柱交相辉映，白色大理石楼梯上方悬挂着中国古典雕漆画。

Magnificent and elegant, the hotel integrates traditional Chinese and modern Western styles. In the lobby stand eight brilliant, gilded columns and over the white marble staircases hang classical Chinese paintings.

例11

学院将立足中国，面向全球，希望与社会各界携手合作，共同服务于国家发展，为国家培养具有“中国情怀、国际视野、社会责任”的全球领袖人才而共同努力。

The school, *based in* China and *oriented to* the world, wishes to cooperate with all circles of society in serving the national development and in producing patriotic global leaders with a great sense of responsibility.

以上两个例子中，例10是饭店介绍，带有宣传的性质；例11是学院介绍，也带有宣传的意味。特别是两个例子中的下划线部分体现了中文背后的审美思维，但是翻译时使用的词就相对简单，例10中的“庄重、富丽、典雅”仅翻译成两个词（magnificent and elegant），“交相辉映”直接省译；例11“立足”和“面向”在英译文中也只是翻译成普通的词组（based in, oriented to）。

中文机构介绍中经常会提到机构的理念，有些理念的表达特别具有感染力，但翻译时要注意适当简化，以符合英语的表达和审美习惯。请看下面的例子：

例12

本公司坚持“以质量和信誉取胜”的方针，实行平等互利的政策，参考国际习惯做法，重合同、守信用，积极发展与世界各大厂商的贸易往来。

With “quality and prestige first” as our principle and mutual benefit as our policy, we aim to develop business with traders all over the world by honoring contracts and international practice and maintaining commercial integrity.

例13

在长期办学历程中，大学形成了“兼容并蓄、博学笃行”的校训精神，成为培养外交、翻译、教育、经贸、新闻、法律、金融等涉外高素质人才的重要基地，一批批毕业生，遍布世界各国、全国各地，活跃于各行各业，建功立业、成就卓著，成为精英翘楚、社会栋梁。

Guided by its motto “Learn with an open mind; Serve a great cause,” the university has, over the years, produced a large number of qualified professionals who work in and outside China as diplomats, translators/interpreters, educators, businessmen/women, journalists, lawyers, bankers, etc.

例14

公司本着“关怀、事业、分享”的企业文化和“信誉第一、客户至上”的企业宗旨，竭诚与国内外广大客商携手共进，共创美好未来。

With the organizational culture of “care, cause and share” and the service philosophy of “reputation and customer priority,” we would like to cooperate with partners from both home and abroad to create a more prosperous future.

从这几个例子来看，机构的方针、原则、理念等具体表述在翻译时尽可能简洁，大多会使用名词短语，当然也不排除使用句子（如例13）。总体来说，这些方针、原则和理念的翻译基本符合英语的表达习惯。

（二）句式特点

中文机构介绍的句子一般会比较长，常使用较短的小分句，读来比较有节奏感，翻译时英语句子不要过于复杂，可使用带有一些短语的简单句或稍微简短的复合句。请看下面的例子：

例15

天津大剧院总建筑面积10.12万平方米，建筑设计立意为“城市舞台”，建筑形式简洁大气、和谐圆润。

Designed as the “City Stage,” Tianjin Grand Theater covers a floor area of 101,200 square meters, featuring a simple and magnificent structure.

例16

酒店内外由名家设计，风格简约、别致，设施齐全，展现的是一个干净、温馨的住宿环境。

Designed by famous architects, the hotel, with simple, unique styles and complete facilities, provides a clean and cozy environment.

以上两个例子原文分别由几个并列结构构成，在翻译时可以找到一个主要结构，其他的次要结构可以通过短语的形式呈现，这种主从结构符合英语的表达特点。

例17

金茂大厦位于上海浦东新区陆家嘴金融贸易区黄金地段，与著名的外滩风景区隔江相望，共88层，高420.5米，堪称上海的一座标志性建筑。

Jin Mao Tower is located in the Lujiazui area of Shanghai's Pudong New Area, facing the Bund across the Huangpu River. This 88-story skyscraper, 420.5 meters high, is known as a landmark of the city.

例18

中华人民共和国成立后，全国高校于1952年进行院系调整，北京大学成为一所以文理基础教学和研究为主的综合性大学，为国家培养了大批人才。

After the founding of the People's Republic of China, a nationwide readjustment of colleges and universities was carried out in 1952. After that, Peking University became a comprehensive university of teaching and research in both liberal arts and science. Since then, it has produced a large number of talented graduates for the nation.

以上两个例句原文中含有多个并列结构，并且可以划分为几个意群，所以无法像例15和例16那样翻译成一句话，而是根据意群拆分为两个或多个英语句子，每个句子长度适中，符合英语机构介绍的句式特点。

（三）修辞特点

中文机构介绍材料善于使用各种修辞手法来提升宣介效果。处理中文机构介绍中的修辞手段时，如果能在英文中找到较为生动的表达方式，则尽可能使用；如果找不到，则不要硬译，特别是"夸张"这种修辞手法，硬译往往达不到表达效果，还适得其反，所以建议直接解释原文的意思，让英文读者清楚地了解原文信息，从而真正实现介绍和宣传的目的。

例19

天津自然博物馆是目前我国早期博物馆中唯一一座原址、原建筑、原藏品、原展柜、原历史文献完整保存至今的博物馆，堪称中国早期博物馆史上的一座"活化石"。

Tianjin Natural History Museum is the only museum among all those early ones in China that has been preserved to today with its original premises, collections, showcases, and historical documents. Therefore, it is known as a living fossil.

例20

40年来，一批批德才兼备的教学、科研和管理人员汇集在这里，怀着振兴教育的希冀，在这片土地上默默耕耘。春华秋实，硕果累累，数万名教育人才走出学校，足迹遍及全国，桃李满天下。

In the past four decades, a large number of talented teachers, researchers, and administrators have gathered and worked here in continuous efforts to meet the ever-increasing demands for educators of China. Tens of thousands of students have graduated from the university, and become teachers in different parts of the country, contributing to the education of the country.

例21

创建于1866年的福建船政学堂，是中国最早的科技专科学校。学堂海纳百川，领风气之先，开中国新式教育之先河，既引进外国先进科技、人才及办学模式，中西合璧，培育新人；又选派优秀学生出洋留学深造。

Founded in 1866, Foochow Shipbuilding Institution was the first polytechnic college in China. It was a pioneer of modern colleges where advanced technologies and new ways of administration from the West were introduced to blend with the best aspects of the Chinese educational system. Many talented students were selected from it to study abroad.

例22

公司诞生于20世纪末，信守孜孜以求、永不言退的发展理念，在市场经济的大潮中，任凭浊浪排空，惊涛拍岸，独有胜似闲庭信步的自信，处变不惊，运筹帷幄。尽握无限商机于掌间，渐显王者之气于天地。

Founded in the late 20th century, the company, adhering to its philosophy of seizing every business opportunity, has achieved its brilliance and become the leader of its industry in the increasingly competitive market.

以上四个例子中，例19的"活化石"属于比喻，这个比喻直译出来能够为英语读者接受，所以选择直译为living fossil。例20中的"在这片土地上默默耕耘""春华秋实，硕果累累"和"桃李满天下"也属于比喻，但这种比喻如果直译，英语母语者会感觉难以理解，所以简化翻译。例21中的"海纳百川，领风气之先"和例22的整个原文都不同程度地使用了夸张手法，直译为英语会显得浮夸，只需要翻译出原文的实质意思。

三、机构介绍翻译原则与策略归纳

综上所述，机构介绍文本的翻译原则可归纳为：(1) 译文用词符合目的语读者对该文体用词的预期，即英译中措辞可以美化一点，中译英要简化一些；(2) 句式灵活处理，英译中使用并列分句结构，中译英使用简单的主从结构；(3) 中文修辞格翻译时要符合英语读者的预期，中文机构介绍中常用的修辞格应避免直译。具体策略归纳可用下表表示：

英译中

	英文机构介绍的文体特点	翻译策略
词汇	用词简单	一般可以直译，但有时要根据中文读者的预期美化措辞，注意用词正式。
	不同领域的专业术语	翻译成汉语对应的专业术语。
句式	简单句、简短的复合句或并列句	翻译时需要注意中文的衔接与连贯，可使用一些小分句。

中译英

	中文机构介绍的文体特点	翻译策略
词汇	表达理念、原则时，用词富有感染力。	一般要根据英语读者的表达习惯进行简化处理，比如转换成名词（结构），有时也会使用分句，要注意行文中的语法。
句式	一般会比较长，中间使用较短的小分句。	翻译时要注意英语句子不要过于复杂，可使用简单句或简短的复合句。
修辞	经常使用比喻、夸张等修辞手法，以达到介绍和宣传机构的目的。	翻译时如果能在英文中找到较为生动的表达方式，则尽可能使用；如果找不到，就不要硬译原文，特别是夸张的修辞手法，建议不直译，只解释原文的意思。

第二模块：英文机构介绍语篇汉译解析

原文

The United Nations (UN) is an intergovernmental organization established on 24 October 1945 to promote international co-operation. A replacement for the League of Nations, the organization was created following the Second World War to prevent another such conflict. At its founding, the UN had 51 Member States; there are now 193.

The UN Headquarters is situated in Manhattan, New York City, enjoying extraterritoriality. Further main offices are situated in Geneva, Nairobi, and Vienna. The organization is financed by assessed and voluntary contributions from its Member States.

Its objectives include maintaining international peace and security, promoting human rights, fostering social and economic development, protecting the environment, providing humanitarian aid in cases of famine, natural disaster, and armed conflict. The UN has six principal organs: the General Assembly, the Security Council, the Economic and Social Council (ECOSOC), the Secretariat, the International Court of Justice, and the Trusteeship Council. UN specialized agencies include the World Bank, the World Health Organization, the World Food Programme, UNESCO, and UNICEF.

The UN's most prominent officer is the Secretary-General. Non-governmental organizations may be granted consultative status with ECOSOC and other agencies to participate in the UN's work. Four principal organs are located at the main UN Headquarters in New York City. The International Court of Justice is located in The Hague. The six official languages of the United Nations, used in intergovernmental meetings and documents, are Arabic, Chinese, English, French, Russian, and Spanish.

翻译解析

本篇是联合国的简介，涉及联合国历史、宗旨、机构组成等。词汇方面涉及联合国的机构名称，句式结构并不复杂，短语使用较为频繁。具体翻译问题解析如下。

1. 联合国机构名称

本篇涉及联合国的机构，有些使用了缩写，这些机构已经有对应的中文翻译，需要查阅资料找到这些译文。本篇出现的联合国机构及其中译文列举如下：

（1）General Assembly：大会

（2）Security Council：安全理事会（简称“安理会”）

（3）Economic and Social Council (ECOSOC)：经济及社会理事会

（4）Secretariat：秘书处

（5）International Court of Justice：国际法院

（6）Trusteeship Council：托管理事会

（7）World Bank：世界银行

（8）World Health Organization：世界卫生组织

（9）World Food Programme：世界粮食计划署

（10）UNESCO：联合国教科文组织（英语全称为United Nations Educational, Scientific and Cultural Organization）

（11）UNICEF：联合国儿童基金会（英语全称为United Nations International Children's Emergency Fund）

2. 其他专有名词

本篇还有一些其他专有名词，包括机构名称和地名，这些专有名词也需要查阅资料找到中文已有的对应翻译。

（1）League of Nations：国际联盟

（2）Manhattan：曼哈顿

（3）New York City：纽约市

（4）Geneva：日内瓦

（5）Nairobi：内罗毕

（6）Vienna：维也纳

（7）The Hague：海牙

3. 语序调整

由于英语句子大多是主从结构，一般说来主结构放在前面，从属结构放在后面，但中文表达多用并列结构，按时间顺序或逻辑顺序进行排列。因此，英译中有时需要调整原文的顺序，才能使译文符合中国读者的表达习惯。

（1）The United Nations (UN) is an intergovernmental organization established on 24 October 1945 to promote international co-operation.

这句话译成中文时最好先译出成立的时间，再说性质。拟译如下：

联合国成立于1945年10月24日，属于政府间国际组织，旨在促进国际合作。

（2）The UN Headquarters is situated in Manhattan, New York City, enjoying extraterritoriality.

这句话可以按照原文的顺序来翻译，但是如果联系下文的意思，最好调整顺序，先写“联合国享有治外法权”，再说“总部设于纽约市曼哈顿”。具体请看下文所讲合句问题和参考译文。

4. 被动语态

本篇有几个句子使用了被动语态。由于中文较少用被动语态，所以这些句子翻译时要转换为中文的主动语态。

（1）A replacement for the League of Nations, the organization was created following the Second World War to prevent another such conflict.

这里create使用了被动语态，但汉语显然不能说“被成立”，直接去掉“被”字即可。整句话拟译为：

其前身为国际联盟，二战后为防止类似冲突再次发生而成立。

（2）The UN Headquarters is situated in Manhattan, New York City, enjoying extraterritoriality.

英语中be located和be situated可以直接译为汉语的主动语态“位于……”，所以整句话可以译为：

联合国享有治外法权，总部设于纽约市曼哈顿。

接下来的一句也是如此，可以照此句进行翻译。

（3）The organization is financed by assessed and voluntary contributions from its Member States.

这句话如果直译为“联合国被……资助”，显然会比较拗口，不如译为“联合国经费来自……”。整句话拟译为：

联合国经费主要来自成员国分摊经费和自愿捐款。

5. 合句

前文曾经讲过，英语机构介绍文本中常使用比较简短的句子，但是前后句子的意思是连贯的，所以这种情况下译成中文需要考虑合句。本篇就有这样的例子：

（1）The UN Headquarters is situated in Manhattan, New York City, enjoying extraterritoriality. Further main offices are situated in Geneva, Nairobi, and Vienna. The organization is financed by assessed and voluntary contributions from its Member States.

这三句话中前两句分别讲联合国总部地址和主要机构的地址，在语义上是连贯的，第三句讲的是联合国经费来源。因此，建议用“联合国”作为主要的视角，将后面两句与第一句合并，中间的句号改为中文的逗号。拟译为：

联合国享有治外法权，总部设于纽约市曼哈顿，在日内瓦、内罗毕和维也纳等地设有办事处，经费主要来自成员国分摊经费和自愿捐款。

这样的译文读起来比较紧凑。试想，如果每一个简单句后面用句号，译文的连贯性会受到影响，读起来也不够舒服。

（2）Four principal organs are located at the main UN Headquarters in New York City. The International Court of Justice is located in The Hague.

这两句话讲的是联合国主要机构的位置，语义也是相连的，因此，建议合句处理。拟译为：

联合国四大主要机构设于纽约市联合国总部，国际法院设于荷兰海牙。

6. 语气

本篇是联合国的介绍，文字比较简单，属于信息类文本。所以，中译文的措辞无需太多渲染，但鉴于是联合国的介绍，所以中译文表达在语气上要正式一些，尽量避免口语化表达。具体请看参考译文。

参考译文

联合国成立于1945年10月24日，属于政府间国际组织，旨在促进国际合作。其前身为国际联盟，二战后为防止类似冲突再次发生而成立。成立之初共有51个成员国，现有193个成员国。

联合国享有治外法权，总部设于纽约市曼哈顿，在日内瓦、内罗毕和维也纳等地设有办事处，经费主要来自成员国分摊经费和自愿捐款。

联合国旨在维护国际和平与安全，促进人权，推动社会经济发展，保护环境，为饥荒、自然灾害和武装冲突提供人道主义援助。其六大主要机构包括联合国大会、安全理事会、经济及社会理事会、秘书处、国际法院和托管理事会，其专门机构包括世界银行、世界卫生组织、世界粮食计划署、联合国教科文组织和联合国儿童基金会。

联合国的行政首长为秘书长。非政府组织可以获得联合国经济及社会理事会和其他机构的咨询地位，参与联合国事务。联合国四大主要机构设于纽约市联合国总部，国际法院设于荷兰海牙。联合国政府间会议和文件共使用六种官方语言，分别为阿拉伯语、汉语、英语、法语、俄语和西班牙语。

第三模块：中文机构介绍语篇英译解析

一

原文

中华艺术宫由2010年上海世博会中国国家馆改建而成，总建筑面积16.68万平方米，展示面积近7万平方米，拥有35个展厅。上海美术馆创建于1956年，是新中国最早建立的美术馆之一，拥有收藏美术精品、开展学术研究、举办陈列展览、普及审美教育、促进国际交流等多项功能，并与海内外著名美术馆建立合作关系。2012年10月1日，上海美术馆迁入原世博园的中国国家馆，并更名为中华艺术宫。馆内还设有艺术剧场、艺术教育长廊等艺术教育传播区域，引进了与馆内整体文化形象相吻合的餐饮、图书、艺术品等配套衍生服务，积极打造"艺术服务综合体"的文化服务概念。

中华艺术宫秉持"艺术服务人民"的立馆宗旨，始终把观众需求作为第一信号，集社会各方之力，加强文化生产，强化公共服务，努力成为公众享受经典艺术、提升艺术美育的高雅殿堂。

翻译解析

本篇是中华艺术宫的介绍和宣传文字，重点在传达实质信息，但也有一些宣传的色彩，翻译时要照顾到英语读者的阅读习惯。

1. 专有名词

本篇涉及一些场馆和机构名称，这些名称要到场馆和机构的相关网站查阅，确认是否已有官方译文。如果有译文就沿用，如果没有译文，就需要自己翻译。本篇主要涉及以下专有名词，大部分都能找到相关译文。

（1） 中华艺术宫：China Art Museum

（2） 2010年上海世博会：the 2010 Shanghai World Expo

（3） 中国国家馆：China Pavilion

（4） 上海美术馆：Shanghai Art Museum

（5） 艺术剧场：Art Theater

（6） 艺术教育长廊：Art Education Corridor

以上六个专有名词中，最后两个没有现成的译文，但可以根据意思进行翻译，将“艺术剧场”译成Art Theater后，可以用搜索引擎反查一下，看英文是否有这样的表达，验证之后便可放心使用。“艺术教育长廊”可借用英语常用的art corridor，中间加上education即可。

2. 渲染词

前文提到，本篇既是介绍性文字，又带有宣传的意味，所以其中不乏渲染语气的词汇，这些渲染语气的词汇需要低调处理，以符合英语读者的预期。

（1）拥有收藏美术精品、开展学术研究、举办陈列展览、普及审美教育、促进国际交流等多项功能。

这里用多个动词并列，表达呈现动态化，实际上也是汉语渲染语气的一种语言手段。但是相对于汉语，英语比较倾向静态表达，因此要考虑省译一些动词。可以联系前文，将前文译为英语的主结构，这一部分用分词短语表示，即serving the purposes of arts collection, academic research, exhibition, aesthetic education, and international communication.

（2）积极打造“艺术服务综合体”的文化服务概念。

这里的“积极打造”无疑属于渲染语气的词，需要低调处理，这句话可以译为：

All these efforts are designed to offer the best artistic and service experience.

（3）集社会各方之力，加强文化生产，强化公共服务，努力成为公众享受经典艺术、提升艺术美育的高雅殿堂。

这里“加强”和“强化”的意思显然一致，因此需要省译一个动词，“高雅”没有必要翻译出来。整个部分拟译如下：

Drawing on social strengths and enhancing cultural production and public service, it tries to be a world where visitors can enjoy classic art and enhance their knowledge about art.

3. 拆句

中文的机构介绍文本会使用带有多个并列分句的长句，中文读者不会觉得复杂，因为小分句读起来比较有节奏感。根据前文关于英语机构介绍文本的句式特点讲解，我们不妨在英语译文中使用一些短语，使得英译文的句子比较简短。如果无法翻译成这样的句子，就要考虑拆句处理。

（1）中华艺术宫由2010年上海世博会中国国家馆改建而成，总建筑面积16.68万平方米，展示面积近7万平方米，拥有35个展厅。

这个句子中“中华艺术宫由2010年上海世博会中国国家馆改建而成”与下文在意思上并不十分连贯，因此考虑拆句处理，将这一部分单独成句。后面可以“拥有35个展厅”为主结构，其他用分词短语。拟译如下：

China Art Museum is what used to be known as China Pavilion of the 2010

Shanghai World Expo. It has 35 exhibition halls covering a floor area of 166,800 square meters and a display area of nearly 70,000 square meters.

（2）上海美术馆创建于1956年，是新中国最早建立的美术馆之一，拥有收藏美术精品、开展学术研究、举办陈列展览、普及审美教育、促进国际交流等多项功能，并与海内外著名美术馆建立合作关系。

这里“并与海内外著名美术馆建立合作关系”与前面的关系并不密切，因此考虑将这一部分单独成句。前面的部分可以将“上海美术馆是新中国最早建立的美术馆之一”作为主句，“创建于1956年”用过去分词，后面的功能前文已经讲过，使用现在分词。拟译如下：

Founded in 1956, Shanghai Art Museum is one of the earliest art museums in China, serving the purposes of arts collection, academic research, exhibition, aesthetic education, and international communication. It has established partnership with art museums at home and abroad.

（3）馆内还设有艺术剧场、艺术教育长廊等艺术教育传播区域，引进了与馆内整体文化形象相吻合的餐饮、图书、艺术品等配套衍生服务，积极打造“艺术服务综合体”的文化服务概念。

这个句子的三个小分句强调了不同的内容，所以翻译时可拆句，即译为三个简短的句子。拟译如下：

The Art Theater and the Art Education Corridor in it introduce knowledge on arts. You can also find food service and book and souvenir shops there. All these efforts are designed to offer the best artistic and service experience.

参考译文

China Art Museum is what used to be known as China Pavilion of the 2010 Shanghai World Expo. It has 35 exhibition halls covering a floor area of 166,800 square meters and a display area of nearly 70,000 square meters. Founded in 1956, Shanghai Art Museum is one of the earliest art museums in China, serving the purposes of arts collection, academic research, exhibition, aesthetic education, and international communication. It has established partnership with art museums at home and abroad. On October 1, 2012, it moved to China Pavilion of the 2010 Shanghai World Expo and the Pavilion was renamed China Art Museum. The Art Theater and the Art Education Corridor in it introduce knowledge on arts. You can also find food service and book and souvenir shops there. All these efforts are designed to offer the best artistic and service experience.

With the philosophy of "art serving the people," China Art Museum takes the demand of the visitors as the top priority. Drawing on social strengths and enhancing cultural production and public service, it tries to be a world where visitors can enjoy classic art and enhance their knowledge about art.

第四模块：翻译练习

1. 英译中

Gavi's impact draws on the strengths of its core partners, the World Health Organization, UNICEF, and the World Bank, and plays a critical role in strengthening primary health care (PHC), bringing us closer to the Sustainable Development Goal (SDG) of Universal Health Coverage (UHC), ensuring that no one is left behind.

Gavi also works with donors, including sovereign governments, private sector foundations, and corporate partners; NGOs, advocacy groups, professional and community associations, and academia; vaccine manufacturers, including those in emerging markets; research and technical health institutes; and implementing country governments.

By improving access to new and under-used vaccines for millions of the most vulnerable children, the Vaccine Alliance is transforming the lives of individuals, helping to boost the economies of lower-income countries, and making the world safer for everyone.

2. 中译英

在上海迪士尼乐园，无论老幼，都可以感受充满创造力、冒险和刺激的乐趣。把目光投向奇幻童话城堡，世界上最大的迪士尼城堡，准备好开始探索这七大各具魅力、令人难忘的神奇园区：米奇大街、奇想花园、梦幻世界、探险岛、宝藏湾、明日世界和迪士尼·皮克斯玩具总动员主题园区。

迪士尼乐园诞生于60多年前，致力于让人们回归纯真，感受快乐，分享难忘经历。如今，上海迪士尼度假区以新颖特别的方式延续着这种精神，打造了全新的主题园区，以及众多独一无二的游乐项目和体验。

第二单元 产品介绍与说明

第一模块：产品介绍与说明翻译概述

产品介绍与说明是生产企业向广大公众和用户介绍、宣传其产品的说明性材料或文书，目的在于让消费者了解产品质量、产品性能、产品的使用方法、使用过程中的注意事项等。所以，产品介绍与说明最大的功能是提供信息。另外，该类文本为读者提供产品使用指南，告诉读者该做什么、不该做什么，因此产品介绍与说明也就具有了指示功能和祈使功能。产品介绍与说明在提供信息和产品使用指导意见的同时，也能激发用户购买产品的欲望，所以也是推销产品的一种方式。当然，产品介绍与说明还可以作为技术人员操作产品的理论依据。产品说明书在语言方面要做到准确无误、简洁清晰、通俗易懂、措辞紧凑，翻译时也要注意保留这些语言特点。

一、英文产品介绍与说明的文体特点及其翻译

（一）用词特点

产品介绍与说明面对的是普通读者，也就是广大的产品用户，因此，英文产品介绍与说明首先要使用普通词汇，显得通俗易懂。例如：

例1

If the light does not go out after the test, or if it illuminates again, have your vehicle inspected at an authorized dealer.

如测试之后灯没有熄灭，或又重新亮起，请将车辆交由授权经销商进行检查。

例2

In order to run the software, put the support software CD-ROM in the CD-ROM drive.

为运行该软件，请在CD—ROM光驱中放入支持CD—ROM的软件。

例3

Do not touch the power cord with a wet hand. Use a soft and dry cloth to clean it.

请勿用湿手触摸电源线，请使用柔软的干布清洁电源线。

仔细阅读上面三例，会发现英语原文的词汇基本都属于普通词汇，通俗易懂，译文基本也使用普通词汇，但措辞显得正式一些。

英文产品介绍与说明中往往使用一些由动词或形容词派生出来的抽象名词做主语，显得比较客观。这些抽象名词译成汉语时一般转译为动词。请看下面的例子：

例4

Operation and *maintenance* of any arc welding equipment involves potential hazards.

<u>操作</u>和<u>维修</u>弧焊接设备存在潜在危险。

例5

Incorrect *connection* of the power cord could result in fire or electric shock.

电源线<u>连接</u>错误可能导致火灾或电击。

例6

Unfamiliarity with the equipment, poor fault *judgment* or *lack* of proper training may cause injury to both the operator and others.

<u>不熟悉</u>设备，<u>判断</u>故障不当，或<u>缺乏</u>正确的培训，都可能会给操作者本人和他人造成伤害。

以上三个例子中的斜体部分都是抽象名词，在译文中都变成了动词，符合汉语的表达习惯。

产品介绍和说明会涉及不同领域的产品，因此常使用相关领域的术语和行话，翻译时尽量在汉语中找到对等的术语。由于一般翻译工作者不可能样样精通，所以应该善于使用各种工具书和参考资料，或求助于专业人士。请看下面的例子：

二

例7

Lamp, *LCD panels*, *polarizing plate* and other *optical components*, and *air filter* and cooling fans have a different lifetime in each.

灯泡、液晶显示屏、偏光板及其他光学元件、空气过滤器和冷却风扇均有各自不同的寿命。

例8

It is a proven basic preparation in cases of *atherosclerotic* and *degenerative* organic diseases associated with old age.

经证实，它是治疗老年动脉粥样硬化和老年器官退化性疾病的基本治疗用药。

例9

Bluetooth is a *wireless protocol* utilizing short-range *communications technology*, facilitating data transmission over short distances from fixed or mobile devices and creating a wireless *personal area network (PAN)*.

蓝牙技术是一种使用短距离无线通信的技术规范，可实现固定设备或移动设备之间的短距离数据传输，创建无线个人局域网。

以上三个例子中斜体部分均为比较专业的术语，这些专业词汇需要译者查阅相关资料，找到汉语对应表达，否则可能会闹出笑话。

另外，英语产品介绍和说明中往往会使用一些缩略语，以体现产品的专业性以及说明书的规范性和简洁性。特别是用于图表或表示技术参数时，更倾向使用缩略语。翻译时，直接找到与这些缩略词相对应的汉语术语即可。下表是英文常用的一些缩略语及其完整表达法和对应的汉语译文：

缩略语	完整词	汉语译文
AC	alternating current	交流电
cal.	calibration	校准
DC	direct current	直流电
dia.	diameter	直径
eff.	efficiency	效率
GP	gauge pressure	表压
I/O	input/output	输入/输出

（待续）

（续表）

缩略语	完整词	汉语译文
ipm	inches per minute	每分钟英寸
L × W × H	Length × Width × Height	长 × 宽 × 高
max	maximum	最大值
REG	regulator	调整器
rpm	revolutions per minute	每分钟转数

（二）句式特点

祈使句是英语产品介绍和说明中最常用的一种句式结构，用来指导用户如何使用产品。这类句子通常可以直译，例如：

例10

After charging, remove the supply unit from the wall socket and pull the small plug out of the appliance.

充电之后，从电源插座上拔下电源部件，并从产品上拔下小插头。

例11

Place the retaining ring back onto the shaving head and turn it clockwise to reattach the retaining ring.

将固定环放回剃须刀头上，然后顺时针旋转以重新安装固定环。

例12

Do not disassemble, install backward, or expose batteries to liquid, moisture, or extreme temperature.

不要拆卸、反向安装电池，不要将电池暴露在液体、潮湿或极端温度之下。

英语产品介绍和说明还常使用if从句，因为产品在使用过程中可能出现这样或那样的情况，条件句可以用来假定一些情况，主句给出解决办法。例如：

例13

If Speed Dialing is set to On, press and hold the Speed Dialing key until the call begins.

如果将单键拨号设为“开”，请按住单键拨号键直到拨出电话为止。

例14

If the needle points toward the minus (-) sign of the scale when the switch is turned on, the battery is being discharged.

点火开关转到通电位置时，指针指在“—”的一侧，表示蓄电池放电。

以上例句中的条件句可以直译为“如果……”，也可以像例14那样译成“……时”。

二、中文产品介绍与说明的文体特点及其翻译

（一）用词特点

中文产品介绍与说明一般用词比较正式，表示产品制造商认真的态度。翻译成英文时注意使用普通词汇。请看下面的例子：

例15

本产品启用前，必须复核电源线路容量，方可使用。

Check the capacity of the power supply before use.

例16

机器运转时请勿靠近。

Do not stay close to the machine when it is in operation.

上述两个例子中“方可使用”和“请勿靠近”在表达上均比较正式。翻译时尽量按照英文产品介绍和说明的词汇特点，选用简单的词汇。

和英文产品介绍与说明一样，中文产品介绍和说明也离不开专业术语。在翻译时需要找到英语中对应的专业术语，切不可乱译。请看下面的例子：

例17

本品副作用与其他青霉素相似，偶可见胃肠道功能紊乱、荨麻疹、皮疹及过敏反应。

As with other *penicillin*, this capsule may cause occasionally *gastrointestinal disturbances*, *urticaria*, *rash*, and *allergic reactions*.

该例中的“青霉素”“胃肠道功能紊乱”“荨麻疹”“皮疹”“过敏反应”都是医学术语。其他医学术语如“药理作用”（pharmacological action）、“适

应症”（indication）、“禁忌”（contraindication）、“副作用”（side effect）等在药品说明书中也频繁使用。

例18

连接交流电源接口路由器的电源线缆时，请使用当地制式的交流电源线缆。

If your *router* uses *AC power supply*, use AC *power cables* in compliance with local *standards*.

该例中下划线的部分均体现了专业特色，翻译时要在英语中使用相对应的专业表达。

中文产品介绍和说明中还使用一些提示语，如“请”“注意”“禁止”“严禁”等字样，这些提示语需要根据其语气选择英语对应的词汇。请看下面的例子：

例19

严禁裸眼直观光纤及光模块出口，以防止激光束灼伤眼睛。

Do not look into bores of optical modules or optical fibers without eye protection since laser beams will cause eye damage.

例20

在安装和维护路由器过程中，请做好防静电保护措施，如佩戴防静电手套或防静电腕带。

Take ESD protection measures during router installation and maintenance. For example, wear ESD gloves or an ESD wrist strap.

例21

绝对禁止同时冲剪两块板材。

Simultaneously cutting two pieces of sheet is strictly forbidden.

以上带有提示语的句子可以译成英语的祈使句，如例19和例20，也可以译成被动语态，如例21。

（二）句式特点

和英文产品介绍与说明一样，中文产品介绍和说明也常用祈使句，提醒用户可以做什么，不能做什么。祈使句可以直译为英语的祈使句，有时也可以译成英语的被动语态。请看下面的例子：

例22

不得将设备置于易燃、易爆气体或烟雾的环境中，不得在这种环境下进行任何操作。

Do not place or operate this product in an environment with flammable or explosive gases, or smoke.

例23

确保设备安装环境空气流通，严禁将设备的散热孔堵塞。

The installation site must be well ventilated. Ensure that air vents on the equipment are not blocked.

以上两个例子原文均为祈使句，英译文有的直接译成祈使句，如例22和例23的后半部分，有的译成了被动语态，如例23的前半部分。

中文产品介绍和说明往往使用较为简单的句式结构，以保证信息的传达简单明了，翻译时也尽量简单。例如：

例24

点击“服务”，可直接查看当前连接的网络和当前机器的IP地址。

Click “Service” and you can check the current network and the machine’s IP address.

例25

采用交互方式输入的密码不会在终端屏幕上显示出来。

The password entered in interactive mode is not displayed on the screen.

例26

本品不适用于丝绸、羊毛、尼龙及皮革制品。

Do not use it on silk, wool, nylon or leather.

中文产品介绍与说明常常使用无主句，以“可以”“必须”“建议”开头。这类无主句可以根据具体情况译成英语祈使句或使用被动语态的陈述句。请看下面的例子：

例27

在墙上打孔时必须确认打孔处的墙中没有电缆，以免触电。

Before drilling holes in a wall, make sure there are no power cables in the wall to avoid electric shock.

例28

如果长时间不使用本产品，或预期天气变化（如雷电天气），则建议将本产品插头取下，以防止遭受雷击而损坏。

If the product remains unused for a long time, or any weather change such as thunder is anticipated, it is recommended that the plug should be taken off so that the product can be protected from thunder shock.

例29

可按照对应的类别搜索电影，如科幻片、动作片、喜剧片、恐怖片、动画片等。

Movies can be selected according to categories, such as science fiction, action, comedy, horror, and cartoon.

和英文产品介绍与说明一样，中文产品介绍和说明也会使用条件句，假设产品可能出现的情况，然后给出解决方案。请看下面的例子：

例30

如不慎入眼，用清水冲洗15分钟；如不慎服用，应立即饮下一杯水或牛奶。两种情况均请医生治疗。

If it is in eyes, rinse with plenty of water for 15 minutes. If it is swallowed, drink a glassful of water or milk. Call the physician in either case.

例31

如果Web用户长时间登录设备但不操作，将占用Web通道资源，致使其他用户无法登录到设备，设置适当的超时时间，可以及时释放Web通道资源。

If a web user logs in to the device but does not perform any operations for a long time, the user occupies web channel resources and other users may fail to log in to the device. You can set a proper time out interval so that web channel resources can be released in a timely manner.

三、产品介绍与说明的翻译原则与策略归纳

英文产品介绍与说明和中文产品介绍与说明都是信息类文体，用词简单，常使用专业术语，同时使用简单句和祈使句，拉近与用户的距离。当

然，中文说明书的语气略显正式。翻译时都尽可能使用简短的句式结构，但英译中时语气要正式一些。具体翻译策略可归纳如下：

英译中

	英文产品介绍与说明的文体特点	翻译策略
词汇	普通词汇	汉语也尽量简单，但语气要正式。
	名词与名词化结构	如果是专业名词，则直译；如果由动词转化来的名词，一般译成汉语的动词，以符合汉语的表达习惯。
	专业术语	译成汉语对应的专业术语，要注意使用工具书或请教专业人士。
	缩略语	汉语说明书一般不使用缩称，所以翻译成汉语完整词汇。
句式	祈使句	通常译为祈使句。
	if 引导的从句	译为带“如果/若”的条件句，有时可省译关联词。

中译英

	中文产品介绍与说明的文体特点	翻译策略
词汇	相对正式的用词	英文注意使用普通词汇。
	专业术语	译为英语的专业术语。
	提示语“请”“注意”等	可译为祈使句；表示“禁止”时可使用被动语态。
句式	祈使句	译为英语祈使句，有时可译为被动语态。
	简单句	译为英语简单句。
	无主句	根据具体情况译成英语祈使句或使用被动语态的陈述句。
	条件句	译为英语条件从句。

第二模块：英文产品介绍与说明语篇汉译解析

原文

This shaver is waterproof. It is suitable for using in the bath or shower and for cleaning under the tap. For safety reasons, the shaver can therefore only be used without cord. The appliance is suitable for mains voltages ranging from 100 to 240 volts.

For maximum shaving performance, we advise you to replace the shaving heads every two years. The appliance is equipped with a replacement reminder which reminds you to replace the shaving heads.

Charge the shaver before you use it for the first time and when the display indicates that the battery is almost empty. Charging takes approx. one hour. When the appliance is fully charged, it has an operating time of 70 minutes.

When charging with the supply unit, make sure the appliance is switched off. Insert the small plug into the appliance and put the supply unit in the wall socket. After charging, remove the supply unit from the wall socket and pull the small plug out of the appliance.

To switch on the appliance, press the on/off button once. To switch it off, press the on/off button once. Your first shaves may not bring you the result you expect and your skin may even become slightly irritated. This is normal. Your skin and beard need time to adapt to any new shaving system.

翻译解析

本篇是剃须刀介绍的一部分，无论是用词还是句式结构均有前文提到的一些现象，翻译时需要注意。

1. 专业术语

（1） cord：电线

（2） mains voltage：电源电压

（3） volt：伏（电压单位）

（4） display：显示器

（5） supply unit：电源部件

（6） plug：插头

（7） socket：电源插座

2. 祈使句

（1）Charge the shaver before you use it for the first time and when the display indicates that the battery is almost empty.

这句话稍微复杂一点，使用了两个时间状语从句，但主结构是祈使句，可以直译为汉语祈使句，当然可以加上“请”字。整句话拟译为：

首次使用前，或者显示屏指示电池电量即将耗尽时，请为剃须刀充电。

（2）When charging with the supply unit, make sure the appliance is switched off. Insert the small plug into the appliance and put the supply unit in the wall socket. After charging, remove the supply unit from the wall socket and pull the small plug out of the appliance.

该段每句话的主结构都是祈使句，均可以直译为祈使句。整段拟译为：

使用电源部件充电时，要确保产品电源已关闭。将小插头插入产品，然后将电源部件插入电源插座。充电之后，从电源插座上拔下电源部件，并从产品上拔下小插头。

（3）To switch on the appliance, press the on/off button once. To switch it off, press the on/off button once.

这两句也都是祈使句，均可以直译为祈使句，但两句话语义连贯，应作合句处理。拟译为：

要打开产品，请按一次开/关键；要关闭产品，请按一次开/关键。

3. 被动语态

本篇有几处使用了被动语态，由于中文少用被动语态，所以翻译时需要转译为主动语态。

（1）For safety reasons, the shaver can therefore only be used without cord.

这里的can be used不适宜译成“能被使用”，建议省译“被”字。拟译为：

出于安全考虑，剃须刀只能在不接电源的情况下使用。

（2）The appliance is equipped with a replacement reminder which reminds you to replace the shaving heads.

这里的is equipped with可以直接译为“配有……”。整句话拟译为：

本产品配有更换提示，会提醒您更换剃须刀头。

（3）When the appliance is fully charged, it has an operating time of 70 minutes.

该句中的从句中使用被动语态，可以直接译为“充满电”。整句话拟译为：

充满电后可持续工作70分钟。

4. 合句

本篇多处句子比较简单，翻译这些简单句并不难，如果这些简单句前后意义连贯，翻译时就需要进行合句处理，以符合中文意合的语言特点。

（1）This shaver is waterproof. It is suitable for using in the bath or shower and for cleaning under the tap.

前后两句意思紧密相关，所以翻译时建议合句。两句合并后，后一句的主语便可以省译。拟译如下：

本剃须刀具有防水性能，可以在沐浴或淋浴时使用，也可以在水龙头下清洗。

（2）Charging takes approx. one hour. When the appliance is fully charged, it has an operating time of 70 minutes.

这两句均与充电相关，而且都涉及时间，因此，建议译文作合句处理，拟译为：

充电约需1小时，充满电后可持续工作70分钟。

（3）Your first shaves may not bring you the result you expect and your skin may even become slightly irritated. This is normal. Your skin and beard need time to adapt to any new shaving system.

这三句讲的是剃须效果，前后意思相连，因此建议合句处理。拟译为：

前几次剃须可能不会带给您预期的效果，而且您的皮肤可能会感到轻度刺激，这属于正常现象，皮肤和胡须需要时间适应新的剃须产品。

参考译文

本剃须刀具有防水性能，可以在沐浴或淋浴时使用，也可以在水龙头下清洗。出于安全考虑，剃须刀只能在不接电源的情况下使用。本产品适合在100－240伏的电源电压下使用。

为获得最佳的剃须效果，建议每两年更换一次剃须刀头。本产品配有更换提示，会提醒您更换剃须刀头。

首次使用前，或者显示屏指示电池电量即将耗尽时，请为剃须刀充电。充电约需1小时，充满电后可持续工作70分钟。

使用电源部件充电时，要确保产品电源已关闭。将小插头插入产品，然后将电源部件插入电源插座。充电之后，从电源插座上拔下电源部件，并从产品上拔下小插头。

要打开产品，请按一次开/关键；要关闭产品，请按一次开/关键。前几次剃须可能不会带给您预期的效果，而且您的皮肤可能会感到轻度刺激，这属于正常现象，皮肤和胡须需要时间适应新的剃须产品。

第三模块：中文产品介绍与说明语篇英译解析

二

原文

感谢您使用AR系列路由器。为保障人身和设备安全，请遵循设备上的标识及手册中的安全注意事项。手册中的“注意”事项，并不代表所应遵循的所有安全事项，只作为安全注意事项的补充。

【注意】：

- AR系列路由器为A级产品，在生活环境中，该产品可能会造成无线电干扰。在这种情况下，可能需要用户对其干扰采取切实可行的措施。
- 请勿在路由器上堆放杂物。
- 不得将设备置于易燃、易爆气体或烟雾的环境中，不得在这种环境下进行任何操作。
- 设备安装环境严禁出现渗水、滴漏、结霜现象，否则需加装除湿设备。
- 确保设备安装环境空气流通，严禁将设备的散热孔堵塞。
- 禁止在高密度灰尘的环境下安装设备。

翻译解析

本篇取自路由器说明书中的“安全注意事项”部分，其中有不少相关专业术语，祈使句也比较多，在翻译时要注意把握语气。

1. 专业术语

（1） 路由器：router

（2） 注意：caution

（3） 无线电干扰：radio interference

（4） 易燃、易爆气体：flammable or explosive gases

（5） 除湿设备：dehumidifier

（6） 散热孔：air vent

2. 祈使句

本篇有多个祈使句，旨在告知用户要做什么，不能做什么，这些祈使句基本都可以直译为英语的祈使句。

（1）为保障人身和设备安全，请遵循设备上的标识及手册中的安全注意事项。

这句话的主结构是祈使句，直接翻译即可。整句话拟译为：

To ensure personal and equipment safety, observe all the safety precautions on the equipment and in this document.

（2）请勿在路由器上堆放杂物。

这句也可以直接译成祈使句：

Do not place other objects on the router.

3. 带有“严禁”和“禁止”等提示语的句子

（1）确保设备安装环境空气流通，严禁将设备的散热孔堵塞。

这句话的后半部分使用“严禁”提示用户不能做什么。可以考虑将前后两句拆分，前面使用被动语态，后面使用祈使句表示强调。拟译为：

The installation site must be well ventilated. Ensure that air vents on the equipment are not blocked.

（2）禁止在高密度灰尘的环境下安装设备。

这句话可以直接译为否定的祈使句，即：

Do not install the equipment in a dusty environment.

4. 无主句

本篇出现了几个无主句，可以根据语境进行处理，有时需要译成英语的被动语态，显得比较客观。

（1）在这种情况下，可能需要用户对其干扰采取切实可行的措施。

这里的“可能需要用户……”是典型的无主句结构，其实际意思为“用户可能需要……”，因此可以译为：

In such a case, the user may be required to take feasible measures.

（2）……否则需加装除湿设备。

这里的“需加装除湿设备”是无主句，可以译成被动语态，即：

Otherwise, dehumidifiers or dehumidifying air conditioners have to be used.

5. 拆句

中文属于意合语言，善于使用小分句，意思完整才能成为一个句子。英语是形合语言，形式完整就是一个句子。此外，英语产品介绍和说明往往使用较为简单的句子。这种对比说明，汉语的产品介绍和说明中有些句子翻译成英语时需要拆分成多个句子。

（1）设备安装环境严禁出现渗水、滴漏、结霜现象，否则需加装除湿设备。

这个句子可以用分号隔开，后面用连接副词otherwise。但是考虑到英语产品介绍和说明句子比较简短，所以建议不用分号，而是拆分成两句。拟译为：

The installation site must be free from leaking or dripping water, heavy dew, and humidity. Otherwise, dehumidifiers or dehumidifying air conditioners have to be used.

（2）确保设备安装环境空气流通，严禁将设备的散热孔堵塞。

这个句子前半部分是肯定的，后面"严禁……"暗含"不得……"这一否定之意，所以最好不要译成一个英文长句，而是拆分成两句。拟译如下：

The installation site must be well ventilated. Ensure that air vents on the equipment are not blocked.

参考译文

Thank you for purchasing an AR series router. To ensure personal and equipment safety, observe all the safety precautions on the equipment and in this document. CAUTION items do not cover all the safety precautions, and are only supplementary to the safety precautions.

CAUTION

- This is a class A product. In a domestic environment this product may cause radio interference in which case the user may be required to take feasible measures.
- Do not place other objects on the router.
- Do not place or operate this product in an environment with flammable or explosive gases, or smoke.
- The installation site must be free from leaking or dripping water, heavy dew, and humidity. Otherwise, dehumidifiers or dehumidifying air conditioners have to be used.

- The installation site must be well ventilated. Ensure that air vents on the equipment are not blocked.
- Do not install the equipment in a dusty environment.

第四模块：翻译练习

1. 英译中

Clean the shaver after every use for optimal performance. Be careful with hot water. Always check if the water is too hot to avoid burning your hands. Never dry the shaving unit with a towel or tissue, as this may damage the shaving heads.

When the shaving unit is rinsed, water may drip out of the base of the shaver. This is normal. We advise you to let the appliance and its attachments dry before you put the protection caps on the attachments or store the shaver in the pouch. Put the protection cap on the shaver to protect it from any dirt accumulation.

The accessories supplied may vary for different products. The box shows the accessories that have been supplied with your product.

2. 中译英

- AR系列路由器可以安装在19英寸标准机柜/机架中，自行采购的机柜/机架须有足够的安装空间。
- 当机柜/机架的方孔条间距不满足要求时，可使用滑道或托盘安装，滑道或托盘需用户自备。
- 带Wi-Fi功能的路由器不推荐在机柜/机架中安装。
- 电源线与信号线缆的间距要大于10厘米。
- 光纤需配合光模块使用。
- 光纤的弯曲半径需大于40毫米。
- 连接接地线缆时请注意M4端连接到设备，M6端连接到保护地。
- 连接交流电源接口路由器的电源线缆时，请使用当地制式的交流电源线缆。

第三单元 广告宣传

第一模块：广告宣传翻译概述

广告有广义和狭义之分。狭义的广告主要是通过各种媒体手段宣传某一产品或服务，即商务广告。广义的广告就是通过传播媒体向大众宣传商品、服务、思想观念、公益事业等等。本教材所涉及的广告宣传主要是商务广告宣传，主要目的在于向大众宣传商品、服务或商业理念，唤起大众购买此商品或服务的意向。

商务广告宣传文本最大的作用就是尽可能地树立产品、服务和企业的最佳形象，赢得最广泛的消费群体，从而获得最大的销售利润。为此，广告文本要准确传达信息，并给人以美的享受，从而激发购买欲。因此，广告文本的功能主要是信息功能、美感功能和祈使功能，这些功能在文字上都会有所体现，包括用词、句式、修辞等。

一、英文广告宣传文体特点及其翻译

（一）用词特点

英文广告宣传类文本用词一般比较简单，因为要照顾到最广大的读者。据英国语言学家利奇（Leech）调查，英文广告语中，单音节词使用得非常频繁，其目的就是让广告简练、通俗、易记，其中动词包括make、come、get、go、know、keep、look、see、need、buy、love、use、take、feel、like、start、taste、save、choose，形容词有new、good、free、fresh、full、sure、clean、crisp、fine、big、great、real、bright、safe、rich。这些词的使用频率大致按照从高到低排列。针对广告语的这一特点，翻译也应该尽量做到简

单，但表达上需要注意符合中国读者的审美预期。比如：

例1

The taste is great.（某咖啡广告）

味道好极了。

例2

Gracefully rounded, designed in pure Art Deco style, the timepiece accompanies elegant ladies around the clock.

腕表采用雅致的圆形造型和最纯粹的装饰艺术设计风格，日夜陪伴优雅的女性。

例3

This unique emerald is enormously valuable not only for its size and perfect color: It is not oiled and has been left in its natural state.

这块独一无二的祖母绿宝石价值连城，不仅因为其尺寸和完美的色彩，更因为它未经油浸，完全保持了纯天然的质地。

仔细阅读原文和译文，会发现原文用词基本比较简单，当然也会有一些描写的色彩，毕竟要宣传产品。相比之下，中译文表现出的宣传和广告意味更浓厚，更加符合中文读者的预期。

英文广告中还经常使用第二人称代词you以拉近和消费者之间的距离，有时需要译为中文的尊称"您"，有时要根据上下文省译。例如：

例4

Along the way, *you* will enjoy the warmest and the most personal service.

自始至终，您将享受最温暖最个性化的服务。

例5

Add the watches and jewelry *you* like most to your favorites list. To do so, click on "Save as favorite" next to the item. *You* can save your personal selection here temporarily.

将最喜爱的腕表和珠宝首饰加入喜爱的商品清单，只需点击商品旁边的"保存为喜爱的商品"按钮，可以将自己挑选的商品暂时保存在这里。

这两个例子中，例4中的you翻译成了中文的尊称"您"，例5中的you则省译。you后面有情态动词can、may和must时，you一般需要省译。

三

（二）句式特点

英语广告和宣传文本一般使用简单的陈述句、非完整句、祈使句等，这样使得行文简单明了，旨在引人注意，翻译时也应该保持译文简短。请看下面的例子：

例6

We are looking forward to surprising you once a year with a preferential offer. Always when you least expect it.

我们将每年为您提供一次特别优惠，为您送上意外的惊喜——总是在您意想不到的时候。

例7

Enjoy and benefit from various personal VIP treatments on your return to one of our boutiques.

再次光临我们的门店可享受专为贵宾提供的各种待遇和优惠。

以上两个例子出自比较正式的广告宣传，例6第一句是简单的陈述句，第二句是非完整句；例7使用了祈使句。这些句式翻译起来难度不大，但要注意中译文的措辞。另外，请注意例6中前后两句话作了合句处理，这样更符合汉语的表达习惯。

英语广告文本大部分句子都非常简单，而且大多会使用非完整句，翻译也没有难度。现举两例：

例8

A work of art—Scotch Whisky

艺术精品——苏格兰威士忌。

例9

Light as a breeze, soft as a cloud.（某服装广告）

轻如微风，柔似彩云。

（三）修辞特点

英语广告宣传往往会使用修辞手法，特别是通过比喻、拟人、反复、双关、设问等修辞手法增强感染力，提升广告宣传效果。上述修辞手法大多可以直译为中文，但是像双关这样的修辞手法有时可以直译，有时可能会比较难翻译，需要根据情况处理。请看下面的例子：

例10

When love strikes like a bolt of lightning and the sparks of love fly: heart-shaped pendant with 33 diamonds.（明喻）

爱犹如一道闪电，释放出爱的火花漫天飞舞：镶有33颗钻石的心形吊坠。

例11

... on Valentine's Day: exquisite pieces of jewelry with all the magic and romance of a beautifully penned love letter.（暗喻）

……情人节：精致的珠宝首饰如同精心书写的情书一样散发着无尽的魔力和浪漫。

例12

Their partnership dates back to 1925, when the brand set out to conquer the watch world.（拟人）

他们的合作关系可以追溯到1925年，当时该品牌刚刚踏上征服腕表世界的旅程。

例13

The brand's philosophy is founded on a simple premise: never be satisfied, never compromise.（反复）

该品牌的理念基于一个简单的前提：永不满足，永不妥协。

例14

There's never been a better *Time*.（双关）

从未有过的好《时代》。

例15

Is it to be that tender loving feeling or endless longing? Take heart and give free rein to your emotions—with a precious piece of jewelry.（设问）

想表达温柔的爱情和永恒的爱慕之情吗？那就选择一款珍贵首饰，然后鼓起勇气，大胆表白吧。

以上例子说明，英语广告宣传中常用一些修辞，这些修辞在翻译时一般都会保留，或者如例11所示，将暗喻转译成了明喻。

三

二、中文广告宣传文体特点及其翻译

（一）用词特点

中文广告宣传类文本用词比较华美，渲染色彩浓厚，翻译时需要根据英语广告词汇的特点进行简化或者“低调处理”，即前文所说英语广告宣传用词简单。请看下面的例子：

例16

金相玉映，品质卓越，格调不凡，身价不菲。宜馈赠，永志良缘；宜珍藏，金吉玉瑞。

With perfect quality and style, it can be both a gift of good wishes and a treasure for good luck.

例17

欢迎加入“外文导游话四季”视频征集活动，在这个舞台上用您的专业，您的热情，您对中国山河大地的深情，向世界发出邀请。

Join the call for video contributions to “Tour China with Me,” where you can show China to the world with your skills and your passion and with your love for the country’s landscapes.

这两个例子原文均使用了描写和渲染语气比较浓重的词，其中例16基本使用偏文言的词汇，例17使用“舞台”“热情”“深情”等，但读者会发现其英译文基本选用的是简单词汇，以符合英语读者的表达习惯，从而实现译文在目的语中的宣传目的，达到宣传效果。因此，翻译广告宣传类文本，要特别注意中英文思维和审美之间的差异。

当然，中文也有一些措辞相对简单的广告词，例如：

例18

家有三洋，冬暖夏凉。（三洋空调广告）

Sanyo warms your winter and cools your summer.

例19

牙好，胃口就好，身体倍儿棒，吃嘛嘛香！（某牙膏广告）

Good teeth, good appetite, good health.

以上两句广告词都使用了简单的词汇，直译成英文也比较通俗易懂，符合英语广告词的用词特点。

（二）句式特点

中文广告宣传的句式基本上是由小分句组成的句子，有些小分句比较简短。翻译成英文时要根据前文讲的广告宣传句式特点进行处理，一般都要简化，有时甚至可以选用非完整句。请看下面的例子：

例20

竹编作为中国传统工艺，有着悠久的历史文化，是中华民族劳动人民辛勤劳作的结晶。

As a traditional Chinese handicraft, bamboo weaving enjoys a long history. It is an embodiment of the hard work of the Chinese people.

例21

和氏璧，价值连城，玉中至尊；金猪玉璧，升值无限，收藏极品。

He Shi Bi, an invaluable jade plate second to none; Gold Pig & Crystal Emerald, a superb choice for collection.

以上两个例子原文都是由小分句组成的，分别译成了两个单句和一个非完整句，基本符合英语广告宣传的句式结构特点。

（三）修辞特点

中文广告宣传也会使用一些修辞手法，包括比喻、拟人、双关、反复、用典、夸张等，这些修辞手法充分体现了中文重审美和艺术的特征。当然，这些修辞手法的运用和前文提到的英文广告一样，目的都是提升广告宣传的效果。上述修辞手法在翻译时要根据具体修辞的情况，如果直译能够为英语读者接受，则可以直译。但像双关、用典和夸张这些修辞手法，大多比较难以直接译成英文，需要根据情况处理，有时可转译为其他修辞手法。请看下面的一些例子：

例22

你是雄鹰，我们给你一片浩瀚的蓝天；你是骏马，我们给你一片辽阔的草原。（某公司人才招聘广告）（暗喻）

If you are an eagle, we are the sky; if you are a steed, we are the grassland.

例23

一切为用户着想，一切为用户负责。（反复）

We do all for you.

例24

“金猪玉璧”一相逢，便胜却人间无数。(用典)

Gold Pig & Crystal Emerald, a perfect match of gold with emerald.

例25

“老城隍庙五香豆”流传至今颇受东南亚华侨之宠爱，生意兴隆，口碑载道，尝者百吃不厌，齿颊留香。(夸张)

Chenghuang Temple Five-flavored Beans have long been popular among the Chinese in Southeast Asia.

以上例子原文采用了不同的修辞手法，包括比喻、反复、用典、夸张，第一种修辞手法基本可以保留，但后三种基本只是翻译了意思。如果直译中文用典，不了解中国文化的读者会感到一头雾水；夸张是中文常用的修辞手段，但英语广告宣传渲染词较少，在翻译时也要注意符合英文的表达习惯。

三、广告宣传翻译原则与策略归纳

由上文的分析可以看出，无论是英文的广告宣传，还是中文的广告宣传，翻译时尽可能语言简洁，但还要突出一定的美感，以符合目的语受众的心理；特别是英译中，更要注重在保持原意的基础上调整措辞，增加渲染词，中译英则有时需要进一步简化。另外，如果使用了包含文化元素的修辞手法，还要注意目的语读者的文化心理，使读者产生文化的认同感，这样才能取得良好的翻译效果和广告效果。所以，有的修辞可以直译，有的则需要变通。广告宣传类文本的具体策略归纳可用下表表示：

英译中

	英文广告宣传的文体特点	翻译策略
词汇	用词简单	一般可以直译，有时要根据中文读者的预期美化一些措辞，注意用词正式。
	使用第二人称代词以拉近和消费者之间的距离。	有时需要译为中文的尊称“您”，有时要根据上下文省译。
句式	一般使用简单的陈述句、非完整句、祈使句等。	翻译时也应该保持译文简短。

（待续）

（续表）

	英文广告宣传的文体特点	翻译策略
修辞	比喻、拟人、反复、双关、设问等	大多可以直译，像双关这样的修辞有时可以直译，有时可能会省译，需要根据情况处理。

中译英

	中文广告宣传的文体特点	翻译策略
词汇	用词比较华美，渲染色彩浓厚。	根据英文广告词汇的特点进行简化，“低调处理”。
	一些广告词措辞相对简单。	对照原文，翻译也可相对简单一些。
句式	小分句使用频繁，一些小分句比较简短。	一般要简化处理，有时可以选用非完整句。
修辞	比喻、拟人、双关、反复、用典、夸张等	如果直译能够为英语读者接受，则可以直译。像双关、用典、夸张这些修辞手法，大多比较难以直接译成英文，需要根据情况处理。

第二模块：英文广告宣传语篇汉译解析

原文

Treat your special clients to the exclusive privilege of a private sales session with a watch and jewelry professional. We can arrange these in discreet surroundings or a private lounge at our own premises, or even organize a presentation in the privacy of your client's hotel room.

Special customers can also make use of our Butler Service. We take care of clients' transfer by limousine from their hotel to our store of their choice, ensure that their needs are looked after by a watch and jewelry expert who speaks their language, and give them an exclusive guided sales tour.

A private guided tour through the workshops of a well-known manufacturer is the perfect way to discover the secrets of the world of watchmaking. Look over the shoulders of master craftsmen at work and marvel at the intricacies of an art that combines traditional skills with state-of-the-art technology. Clients will also have a unique opportunity to purchase the watch of their dreams.

Surprise your esteemed clients with a unique Diamond Cocktail Party, an exciting and exclusive event that gives one lucky participant the chance to win a real diamond. A gemologist is on hand to examine each client's stone and announces the winner later on. This is an evening that is guaranteed to delight your very best clients.

Selected clients qualify for the Privilege Voucher, a preferential offer that entitles them to a 10% reduction on purchases totaling 2,000 Swiss francs or more.

翻译解析

本篇是国外某一奢侈品牌公司向客户宣传其服务的文案，行文基本符合英语广告宣传的文体特点，用词比较简单，句式结构不是特别复杂，但有些句子稍长。

1. 措辞

本篇用词大多比较简单，没有太多渲染性词汇，符合英语广告宣传的用词特点，但是译成中文时，措辞要符合中国读者的审美预期，所以要显得正式并表现一定的美感。

(1) Clients will also have a unique opportunity to purchase the watch of their dreams.

这里的dreams用法巧妙，但是如果简单地翻译成“梦”，中文就显得过于简单和直白，不如将the watch of their dreams译成“梦寐以求的腕表”。整句话拟译为：

客户还有难得的机会购买他们梦寐以求的腕表。

(2) This is an evening that is guaranteed to delight your very best clients.

我们知道，delight就是“让人高兴”的意思，但是如果直译为“让客户高兴”，在美感程度上显然不足，所以建议整句话译为：

这样的夜晚一定会令您尊贵的客户喜出望外。

2. 敬称“您”的使用

本篇旨在向客户公司宣传自己的服务，里面出现了几处your，指的是对方公司，所以按照前文所讲，如果译成中文，就需要用尊称“您的”。

(1) Treat your special clients to the exclusive privilege of a private sales session with a watch and jewelry professional.

这里的your显然指的是对方公司，所以不能省译，因此整句话拟译为：

腕表和珠宝专家为您的特殊客户提供专属个性化销售服务。

(2) Surprise your esteemed clients with a unique Diamond Cocktail Party ...

这里的your也不能省译，所以整句话拟译为：

钻石鸡尾酒会一定会为您的尊贵客户送上一份惊喜……

3. 长句

本篇有些句子稍长，如前文所讲，中文广告宣传多使用小分句，所以在翻译时可以将稍长的英文句子进行拆分。

(1) We can arrange these in discreet surroundings or a private lounge at our own premises, or even organize a presentation in the privacy of your client's hotel room.

这个句子中间只有一个逗号，翻译时建议进行拆分，不妨译为：

我们可将个性化销售安排在私密的环境中，或者安排在我们店铺的私人休息室，甚至还可以在您客户所在的宾馆房间内提供私密化展示和销售服务。

(2) We take care of clients' transfer by limousine from their hotel to our store of their choice, ensure that their needs are looked after by a watch and jewelry expert who speaks their language, and give them an exclusive guided sales tour.

这句话有三个动词并列，中文也分别译为三个小分句。整句话译文如下：

我们可以用豪华轿车将客户从宾馆接往他们选定的门店，懂客户母语的腕表和珠宝专家会时刻倾听客户的需求，为他们提供专享的导购服务。

(3) Surprise your esteemed clients with a unique Diamond Cocktail Party, an exciting and exclusive event that gives one lucky participant the chance to win a real diamond. A gemologist is on hand to examine each client's stone and announces the winner later on. This is an evening that is guaranteed to delight your very best clients.

这一段的前后内容在语义上是相连的，所以原文虽然是三句话，但中文建议合并成一句，将原文的每一句都以小分句的形式呈现。拟译如下：

钻石鸡尾酒会一定会为您的尊贵客户送上一份惊喜，这项激动人心的独特活动为每位参加者提供了赢取一枚真钻石的机会，宝石专家会为每位客户的钻石做现场检测并在稍后宣布获胜者，这样的夜晚一定会令您尊贵的客户喜出望外。

参考译文

腕表和珠宝专家为您的特殊客户提供专属个性化销售服务。我们可将个性化销售安排在私密的环境中，或者安排在我们店铺的私人休息室，甚至还可以在您客户所在的宾馆房间内提供私密化展示和销售服务。

特殊客户还可以享受我们的管家式贵宾服务。我们可以用豪华轿车将客户从宾馆接往他们选定的门店，懂客户母语的腕表和珠宝专家会时刻倾听客户的需求，为他们提供专享的导购服务。

在专家的陪同下对著名腕表制造商的工场进行私密的参观，这是了解腕表制造业秘密的绝佳方式。现场观看技艺精湛的大师们工作，感受融合了传统技艺和现代技术的艺术品所带来的震撼。客户还有难得的机会购买他们梦寐以求的腕表。

钻石鸡尾酒会一定会为您的尊贵客户送上一份惊喜，这项激动人心的独特活动为每位参加者提供了赢取一枚真钻石的机会，宝石专家会为每位客户的钻石做现场检测并在稍后宣布获胜者，这样的夜晚一定会令您尊贵的客户喜出望外。

精心挑选的客户有资格获得特别优惠券，凭此券购物满2000瑞士法郎，即可享受10%的优惠折扣。

第三模块：中文广告宣传语篇英译解析

原文

作为一款集红旗品牌最新设计理念和前瞻技术于一体的划时代产品，红旗H9以五大超越创新，奠定新时代新红旗设计灵魂，以九大顶级技术，奉献客户专属愉悦体验，尊享极致驾乘乐趣，树立当代中国汽车产业C+级车全新标杆。

在设计上，该车将优秀传统文化与现代科技深度融合，引领豪华轿车新潮流；同时，首创的“东方意境”座舱，尽显东方智慧，从独创的“一键舒躺”到独具一格的“馥兴之韵”专属香氛，以及首创的旗舰先进技术底盘和动力总成平台，为用户带来越级享受；红旗H9高度智能化，首创智能网联技术Smile 1.0，聚合了自动驾驶、智联生态AI引擎、五屏联动、贴心语音助手、全场景远程控车等多项技术，以实力领潮智能汽车未来；在安全上，红旗H9通过搭载无界视域系统、GUARD安全系统、Safe Plus信息安全系统，以及健康环境系统，开创了国宾级安全。

翻译解析

本篇是红旗轿车H9的广告宣传，体现了中文广告宣传的措辞特色，翻译时要注意如何实现英语广告宣传的效果，很多时候不能拘泥于原文的表达。

1. 专业术语

本篇涉及一些汽车技术以及其他技术的专业词汇，需要在英语中找到对应的表达。

（1）C+级车：C+ class luxury sedan

（2）底盘：chassis

（3）动力总成平台：powertrain platform

（4）智能网联技术：intelligent connection technology

（5）自动驾驶：automatic driving

（6）AI引擎：AI engine

（7）五屏联动：five-screen linkage

（8）语音助手：voice assistant

（9）全场景远程控车：panoramic remote control

（10）无界视域系统：unbound vision system

2. 渲染词

本篇集中展现了中文广告宣传文本的语言特点，里面有很多渲染语气、美感十足的表达。这些渲染语气的词汇不能直接翻译，需要“低调处理”。

（1）奠定新时代新红旗设计灵魂

这里的“奠定……灵魂”显然属于渲染词，如果直译出来就是lay a foundation for the spirit，这种译文语义不清，所以建议转换成lay a foundation for the design。

（2）尊享极致驾乘乐趣

这一部分与前面的“奉献客户专属愉悦体验”意思基本相似，所以可以合并处理，译为offer the passengers unique taking and driving experience。

（3）独具一格的“馥兴之韵”专属香氛

这里的“‘馥兴之韵’专属香氛”如果直译，英语读者将难以理解，所以建议简化。该部分拟译为：“air refreshing” system。

3. 长句

本篇一共两段，每一段都是一句话，句式结构具有典型的汉语句式特点，句子比较长，由多个小分句构成，意思结束才会用句号。这些句子译成英文时要注意不要使用过于复杂的句式结构，该使用短语的时候要使用短语，该断句拆分时就拆分成英文的简单句。

（1）作为一款集红旗品牌最新设计理念和前瞻技术于一体的划时代产品，红旗H9以五大超越创新，奠定新时代新红旗设计灵魂，以九大顶级技术，奉献客户专属愉悦体验，尊享极致驾乘乐趣，树立当代中国汽车产业C+级车全新标杆。

这句话翻译时可以将最后的部分“树立当代中国汽车产业C+级车全新标杆”单独成句，一方面使得前后句子缩短，另一方面也是有强调广告宣传的意味。前半部分的主结构是“红旗H9奠定新时代新红旗设计灵魂，以九大顶级技术，奉献客户专属愉悦体验，尊享极致驾乘乐趣”，主结构谓语动词并列，前面可以用as短语。整句话拟译为：

As a milestone product combining state-of-the-art design and proactive technology of Hongqi, H9 lays a foundation for the design of new Hongqi vehicles in the new era with its five innovations, and offers the passengers unique taking and driving experience with its nine top technologies. It sets a new benchmark in C+ class luxury sedan segment.

（2）在设计上，该车将优秀传统文化与现代科技深度融合，引领豪华轿车新潮流；同时，首创的“东方意境”座舱，尽显东方智慧，从独创的“一键舒躺”到独具一格的“馥兴之韵”专属香氛，以及首创的旗舰先进技术底盘和动力总成平台，为用户带来越级享受；红旗H9高度智能化，首创智能网联技术Smile 1.0，聚合了自动驾驶、智联生态AI引擎、五屏联动、贴心语音助手、全场景远程控车等多项技术，以实力领潮智能汽车未来；在安全上，红旗H9通过搭载无界视域系统、GUARD安全系统、Safe Plus信息安全系统，以及健康环境系统，开创了国宾级安全。

这句话很长，实际上中间的分号说明各部分形式上相对独立，意思上虽有关联但又不十分密切，因此最简单的办法就是将分号隔开的分句转译为独立的四个英文句子，为每一句英文找到一个主结构，其余用短语表示。整句话拟译如下：

In design, H9 is a leader of limousines integrating traditional Chinese culture with modern technology. Its “oriental artistic concept” seat embodies oriental wisdom and its “lying down with one click,” “air refreshing” systems and original chassis of start-of-the-art technology and powertrain platform offer superb enjoyment. Hongqi H9 is a pioneer of intelligent cars, equipped with the Smile 1.0 system, an exclusive intelligent connection technology, involving automatic driving,

AI engine, five-screen linkage, voice assistant, and panoramic remote control. Carrying an unbound vision system, GUARD safety system, Safe Plus information security system, and health & environment system, it brings the passenger the state guest-level security.

参考译文

As a milestone product combining state-of-the-art design and proactive technology of Hongqi, H9 lays a foundation for the design of new Hongqi vehicles in the new era with its five innovations, and offers the passengers unique taking and driving experience with its nine top technologies. It sets a new benchmark in C+ class luxury sedan segment.

In design, H9 is a leader of limousines integrating traditional Chinese culture with modern technology. Its "oriental artistic concept" seat embodies oriental wisdom and its "lying down with one click," "air refreshing" systems and original chassis of start-of-the-art technology and powertrain platform offer superb enjoyment. Hongqi H9 is a pioneer of intelligent cars, equipped with the Smile 1.0 system, an exclusive intelligent connection technology, involving automatic driving, AI engine, five-screen linkage, voice assistant, and panoramic remote control. Carrying an unbound vision system, GUARD safety system, Safe Plus information security system, and health & environment system, it brings the passenger the state guest-level security.

第四模块：翻译练习

1. 英译中

The brand is pleased to present a new ensemble of timepieces for women, the Diamantissima collection. Five models in a range of sizes display a feminine look and feel with elegantly understated detailing. Each watch showcases the iconic diamante pattern, inspired by the brand's famous canvas fabric print featuring a distinctive crisscross motif. These timepieces, with their refined case and minimalist dial, show off this design to its fullest expression: The cases are etched with the diamante pattern, and dials feature the motif all over conveying a fabric print effect. With its understated allure, the Diamantissima watch collection represents a new, refined timepiece for the modern woman.

2. 中译英

作为家喻户晓的中国知名腕表品牌，承袭品牌皇冠LOGO所赋予的王者风范和贵族精神，它以精湛制表工艺和匠心美学，不断设计出众多引领潮流、屡获赞誉的畅销腕表，品牌年销量超过200万只，并对中国腕表行业产生了深远的影响。

从上世纪90年代在中央电视台开创全新品牌推广模式开始，到在钟表行业掀起聘请品牌形象代言人之风潮；从首度试水品牌微电影营销，到以明星全国巡演形式开启行业品牌推广新思路，多年来，它始终以敢为天下先之魄力，引领行业潮流及风尚，推动了中国腕表行业的不断发展及变革。

第四单元 商务期刊

第一模块：商务期刊翻译概述

商务期刊文章是指有关金融、贸易、财政、市场、创业、管理等题材的叙述或评论性文本，一般包括报纸、商务类杂志以及其他商务类读物中的新闻报道、综述、分析评论、专业论文、案例分析、年度报告等。这类文章旨在为人们提供信息、知识和案例，因此具有信息功能，即读者通过阅读该类文章就可以获得有关上述商务领域的信息。中英文商务期刊文章通常使用叙述性或议论性话语，语气比较正式，也比较客观，用词比较正规，语法和句式比较规范。有的文章说明性、概括性较强，有的专业性论文则彰显出较强的学术性。翻译此类文章，一般需要忠实传达原文的信息，注意措辞要客观规范。

一、英文商务期刊文体特点及其翻译

（一）用词特点

商务期刊文章涉及不同的领域，所以会包含各个商务领域的专业词汇，即专业术语，如管理学术语、投资术语、营销术语等等，不一而足。这些专业术语在汉语中一般都能找到对应的表达，所以需要译者掌握一定量的汉语商务术语，当然，也可以在翻译过程中查阅资料，切忌随意翻译。请看下面的例子：

例1

Since *profit rates* were falling in some big, *basic sectors of the economy*, corporations tried for quicker and larger *returns* by investing in *retail*, *services*, and *financial speculation.*

由于某些大型基础经济部门利润率开始下降，各公司纷纷投资零售业、服务业和金融投机业以期获取更快更高的收益。

例2

Leading indicators such as *purchasing managers' indices* suggest that the *euro zone*'s *manufacturing sector* is contracting at an accelerating rate.

采购经理指数等领先指标显示，欧元区的制造业正在加速收缩。

例3

In difficult times, whether you need to *liquidate risky assets* at depressed prices will depend on your expenses and on your other *holdings* of less risky, *salable assets.*

困难时期，是否需要压价清理风险资产取决于自己的消费以及其他低风险可售资产的持有数额。

例4

For example, a manufacturer of basic materials and its major *distributor* work closely to revamp their shared *supply chain.*

譬如，基础材料的生产商及其主要分销商密切合作，改变共享的供应链。

以上四个例子中，英文斜体词汇来自不同领域，包括宏观经济、营销、金融等，需要根据上下文在中文中寻找对应的表达法，体现译文的专业性。

为显示所述内容的准确性和可靠性，英语期刊文章中有时还会出现一些新闻报道用语或引述某人观点的词汇，如according to ...、some believe that/it is believed that ...、as ... point out、sb. says ...、it is reported that ... 等，这些表达翻译成汉语时很容易找到对等的表达方式，如“根据……”“有些人认为……”“正如……指出”“……说/表示/透露”“据报道……”等。请看下面的例子：

例5

The car company *said* yesterday it plans to boost its manufacturing capacity in Shanghai by 50%, expanding its push into the luxury end of the world's fastest growing auto market.

该汽车公司昨日表示，计划在上海增加50%的制造能力，拓展其在世界增长最快的汽车市场中的豪华汽车业务。

例6

Some *believe* that Chinese brands could become a global phenomenon within a decade, marketed on quality and exotic appeal as well as competitive price.

有些人认为，由于质量上乘，风格独特，价格极具竞争力，中国品牌十年内会成为全球性品牌。

例7

According to relevant officials, the company entered into the partnership with them because they are more open to technology transfers than most other industry leaders.

有关人士透露，该公司与他们建立合作关系是因为他们在技术转让方面比该行业中其他大多数领军企业更具开放性。

以上三个例子中，例5中的said译为“表示”，比直译为“说”更正式；例6中的believe译成“认为”，没有译成“相信”；例7中的according to显然不能译成“根据”，译成“透露”更符合上下文的意思。

（二）句式特点

英语商务期刊文章的句式相对比较简单，大多使用简单句，即使使用复合句，句式结构一般也不会过于复杂。请看下面的例子：

例8

Qualifying for a loan can mean the difference between beginning your life as a small business owner and waiting years for your dreams to come true. Bad credit can be one of the biggest hurdles for hopeful entrepreneurs. Thankfully, business loans for bad credit do exist and with a little guidance, today's small business owners can get the boost they need to get their companies up and running.

有资格获得贷款意味着自己作为小企业主的生活开始了，而不用再等待数年才能实现梦想。不良信用可能会是最大障碍之一，妨碍自己成为有前途的企业家；但幸运的是，确实存在为不良信用提供的商业贷款，如今的小企业主在一定的指导下，可以获得自己所需要的资助，从而让公司运转起来。

例9

Of all a company's functions, marketing has perhaps the most to gain from artificial intelligence. Marketing's core activities are understanding customer needs, matching them to products and services, and persuading people to buy—capabilities that AI can dramatically enhance. No wonder a 2018 McKinsey analysis of more than 400 advanced use cases showed that marketing was the domain where AI would contribute the greatest value.

在公司的所有职能中，市场营销或许是从人工智能中受益最多的职能。市场营销的核心活动在于了解客户需求，将客户与产品和服务联系起来，说服大众购买产品，这些功能可以通过人工智能大大增强。麦肯锡咨询公司2018年对400多个人工智能高级应用案例进行了分析，分析表明，市场营销是人工智能体现最大价值的领域，这不足为奇。

这两个例子原文均取自英文期刊，其中句子相对比较简单，例8大多是简单句，只有最后一句是并列句；例9一共有三个句子，第一句是简单句，后面两个句子是复合句，理解难度都不大。其中，例8有些简单句前后意思相连，因此翻译时需要合句处理。例9的最后一个句子稍微复杂一点，这句话的主语（a 2018 McKinsey analysis of more than 400 advanced use cases）比较长，所以要考虑像参考译文那样译成一个分句（麦肯锡咨询公司2018年对……进行了分析），另外句子开头的no wonder建议调整语序，放在译文最后。

二、中文商务期刊文体特点及其翻译

（一）用词特点

首先，中文商务期刊文章也会使用一些专业词汇，这些词汇需要在英文中找到贴切准确的对应语。请看下面的例子：

例10

力争销售额（税后）500万—800万元人民币，主要推广防护工装、防电弧服以及户外服这类成熟产品。

We will work for the (after-tax) *sales value* of RMB five million to eight million to mainly promote the mature products of *preventive work suit*, *anti-arc suit*, and *outdoor suit*.

例11

中央重点支持中西部地区，适当兼顾东部部分困难地区。采取“分项目、按比例”分担的方式，是为了分清中央与地方的经费分担责任，以避免中央与地方责任不明确、信息不对称等问题，是义务教育经费保障的新形式。

The central government gives priority to the middle and west regions, but will not ignore poor areas in the east. The method of financial sharing *by project and by proportion* will be adopted to clarify the responsibilities for financing between the central and the local governments to avoid unclear responsibility or inadequacy of information. Therefore, it is a new form of fund guarantee for *compulsory education*.

例12

但从中国商业零售业的业态分布看，传统大型商场所占比重较大，目前依然是消费品市场的零售主力军。然而近几年连锁超市、专卖店、仓储店也发展迅速，大有与百货商店平分秋色的态势。

However, the structure of China's *retail industry* indicates that large traditional department stores are still the main player, representing a significant proportion of the whole industry. In recent years, however, *chain supermarkets*, *specialty stores*, and *megastores* have developed at an alarming rate, snatching a large slice of the retail pie from department stores.

以上三个例子中，例10中的“销售额”和“防护工装”“防电弧服”“户外服”，例11中的“分项目、按比例”和“义务教育”，例12中的“零售业”“连锁超市”“专卖店”和“仓储店”均属于比较专业的表达，译文都一一对应。

其次，中文期刊文章中会出现“据悉……”“据报道……”“根据……调查”“据预计……”“统计数据显示……”“从……处了解到……”“……指出”等等，这些表达方式在英文中基本能找到对应的表达方法，如as is reported ...、it is reported ...、according to the survey ...、it is estimated ...、statistics show that ...，以及it is learned from ... that ...等等。例如：

例13

据德国媒体报道，欧洲空客公司将废除目前的每周35小时工作制，而将其延长至40小时。

As is reported by German media, European Airbus will abolish its mechanism of 35 work-hours per week and prolong them to 40.

例14

记者从福建省证券期货业协会了解到，福建计划在3月份出台投资者教育工作方案，并力争在4月份实施。

It is learned from the Securities & Futures Association of Fujian that the province will work out an investor education scheme in March and try to put it into effect in April.

例15

根据商务部发布的《中国电子商务报告2017》的数据，2017年，我国跨境电子商务进出口商品总额达到902.4亿元，同比增长80.6%。

According to E-commerce in China (2017) issued by the Ministry of Commerce, the total import and export volume of cross-border e-commerce reached 90.24 billion *yuan* in 2017, with a year-on-year growth of 80.6 percent.

上述三个例子中，“据德国媒体报道”“记者从……了解到”和“根据……的数据”分别译成了as is reported by German media、it is learned from ...和according to ...。

（二）句式特点

中文商务期刊文章中无主句使用较多，这是因为无主句不说出动作的发出者，可以加强所提供商务信息的客观性。由于英语句子一般都是主谓结构，所以翻译时有时需要转换成被动语态，有时根据情况添加主语，使用主动语态。请看下面的例子：

例16

未来，应围绕经济和社会网络化、数字化、智能化发展方向，加快构建高速、移动、安全、泛在的新一代信息基础设施，为推动供给侧结构性改革、构建良好社会秩序提供强有力的网络支撑。

The new-generation high-speed, mobile, secure, and ubiquitous information infrastructure should be constructed for networking, digitalization, and intelligent development of economy and society, to provide strong support for the supply-side structural reform and good social order.

例17

如果为防止可能出现的通胀状况动用利率政策——加息，那么很可能将挤破资产价格泡沫，并不利于经济的持续增长。

If the interest policy—interests increase—is adopted to prevent the possible inflation, the asset price bubble will be probably broken, which will be unfavorable for the steady growth of the economy.

例18

迫切需要进一步利用信息技术提升监管能力，实现对金融的全场景、全链条、全流程的动态监管，使金融科技更好地助力防范国家金融风险，保障国家金融安全，推动新金融发展。

There is an immediate need to make use of IT to improve the supervision capability, so that supervision can cover all financial scenarios, chains, and processes. In this way, financial technology can better prevent national financial risks, guarantee national financial security, and promote the development of new finance.

以上三个例子的主结构都是无主句，前两个根据情况翻译成了英语的被动语态，例18依然使用主动语态，运用了there be 结构。实际上，无论是使用被动语态还是there be 结构的主动语态，语气都比较客观，跟原文相符。

中文商务期刊文章中有一些句子比较长，中间用逗号分开，即小分句并列，翻译时要注意分析句子结构，判断是否可以译为英语的一句话。如果译成一句话过于复杂，就需要拆句处理，因为如前文所说，英语商务期刊文章的句子大多不长。请看下面的例子：

例19

善待竞争者，做自己的事，用“没有最好只有更好”这种观念来引领市场，主导市场，这是企业的宗旨也是奋斗的方向和目标。

It is the philosophy and goal of a company to treat the rivals kindly, do what the company should do, and lead the market through the idea that there is no best but ever better product.

仔细分析这句话，会发现其主语是“善待……主导市场”，包含四个小分句，后面“是企业的宗旨也是奋斗的方向和目标”可以处理为英文系表结构，但由于主语包含四个动词，如果使用四个连续的不定式短语放在句首，显得太长，因此可以用it做形式主语。

例20

专家分析说，新条例实施后，今后从事特许经营行业，至少拥有两个直营店，经营时间超过一年，这样一来可以有效防止一些企业利用特许经营进行欺诈，有利于规范整个特许经营行业的发展。

Experts hold that after the new regulations are put into force, the industries with licensed operation shall have at least two retail stores which shall have been in business for at least one year. Thus cheating through licensed operation can be prevented, which will be favorable to the development of the entire licensed operation industry.

这一中文长句由多个并列分句构成，很难译为一个英文长句，应拆句处理。不妨根据逻辑关系在“经营时间超过一年”后面断开，拆分成两句话，第一句话陈述事实，第二句话讲述新条例实施带来的影响。

三、商务期刊翻译原则与策略归纳

综上所述，商务期刊文章的翻译原则可归纳为以下几点：(1) 术语使用得当。商务期刊文章会涉及经济、商业、管理等方面的内容，因此会有一些相关的术语，翻译时需要找到对应的表达，术语翻译得当能够在一定程度上保证译文的专业性。(2) 句式结构灵活处理。由于英语商务期刊文章通常用比较简短的句子，但相邻的句子意思往往紧密相关，因此需要合句处理；而中文长句较多，包含多个小分句，译成英语时尽量使用简单句，个别情况下需要拆句处理。(3) 把握原文的语气。中英文商务期刊文章一般带有一定的学术性，行文和措辞比较正式，翻译时需要把握这种语气。商务期刊文章具体翻译策略可归纳为下表：

英译中

	英文商务期刊的文体特点	翻译策略
词汇	使用不同商务领域的专业术语。	翻译成汉语对应的专业术语。
	使用反映准确性和客观性的新闻报道用语。	翻译成汉语中反映准确性和客观性的新闻报道用语。
句式	使用简单句和复合句。	分析句子结构，找出逻辑关系，根据汉语的表达习惯将信息进行重组，但保证意思不变。

中译英

	中文商务期刊的文体特点	翻译策略
词汇	使用不同商务领域的专业术语。	翻译成英语对应的专业术语。
	使用反映准确性和客观性的新闻报道用语。	翻译成英语中反映准确性和客观性的新闻报道用语。
句式	使用无主句。	根据上下文或说话的语气添加主语，译为主动语态；有时为再现客观语气，可译为被动语态。
	使用并列结构组成的长句。	有的可以译成一个英语长句，有的可根据意群拆句，译成多个英语简单句。

第二模块：英文商务期刊语篇汉译解析

原文

When you meet with investors of any sort, they are likely to ask questions designed to expose your vulnerabilities—operational, financial, and competitive. They will also probe your oversight of the management team. They want to satisfy themselves that you are managing talent, strategy, and risk to enhance shareholder returns, whether for short-term gain or long-term value.

Investors might also ask how you prepare for succession, both in the company and on the board, and how you ensure that the company is building the capabilities needed for sustained growth. In addition, they will want to know how you are developing sources of information so that you can make independent judgments about the market for talent. You should also be ready to discuss executive compensation. The level of pay, along with the types of compensation and the triggers for enhanced rewards, will tell investors whether the company is emphasizing short- or long-term growth or balancing the two. For instance, annual bonuses and rewards often rise in tandem with the stock price; that's normal. But if the CEO gets a 200% bonus for exceeding the target price, that's a driver of short-termism. And if the company wants to pull money from the future to meet short-term goals, investors will want to know whether management must first seek board approval.

Investors will be curious, too, about the board's operations. They will also ask questions related to social impact. You can be certain your investors are looking for insights about what metrics the board uses to assess performance, along with information about incentives and stock ownership levels among managers.

四 翻译解析

这是一篇关于投资人与公司关系的期刊文章，里面有一些专业的商务术语，大多数句子比较简单，但也有稍微复杂的句子。虽然很多句子使用了you做主语，但整篇语气比较正式。下面就对本篇翻译要注意的问题进行解析。

1. 专业术语

本篇谈及的问题比较专业，里面有一些词汇涉及投资及企业管理这样的专业领域，所以需要译者学习并记住相应的中文表达。详列如下：

（1） shareholder return：股东收益

（2） short-term gain：短期收益

（3） long-term value：长期价值

（4） board：董事会

（5） sustained growth：持续增长

（6） executive compensation：管理人员薪资

（7） annual bonus：年度奖金

（8） stock ownership：持股/股权

2. 长句

本篇有一些稍复杂的句子，翻译时需要注意分析，适时地译成由多个小分句构成的句子。请看下面的例子：

（1）When you meet with investors of any sort, they are likely to ask questions designed to expose your vulnerabilities—operational, financial, and competitive.

这句话要注意破折号后面的三个形容词是修饰vulnerabilities的，译成汉语时不必都提到前面，否则修饰语会显得太长，放在后面补充说明即可。另外，破折号可以省略。整句话拟译如下：

与任何类型的投资人见面，他们都可能会提出一些问题来发现你公司存在的不足，包括经营业绩、财务状况、竞争优势等方面存在的不足。

（2）They want to satisfy themselves that you are managing talent, strategy, and risk to enhance shareholder returns, whether for short-term gain or long-term value.

这句话翻译前需要分析一下，其中主句是They want to satisfy themselves that ...，可翻译为“他们想确认……”，后面是宾语从句；to enhance ...是目的状语，翻译时可以提前；最后由whether引导的从句起到补充说明的作用，可以考虑放在括号里。整句话拟译为：

他们想确认：为提高股东收益（无论是获得短期收益还是长期价值），你在有效管理人才，实施战略，控制风险。

（3）In addition, they will want to know how you are developing sources of information so that you can make independent judgments about the market for talent.

这句话是一个复杂句，其中so that引导的从句做目的状语，翻译时可以从这里断开，用一个小分句来表达目的。整句话拟译为：

此外，他们还想知道你如何开发信息资源，以便你对人才市场做出独立判断。

（4）The level of pay, along with the types of compensation and the triggers for enhanced rewards, will tell investors whether the company is emphasizing short- or long-term growth or balancing the two.

这句话的主语部分由the level of pay和the types of compensation and the triggers for enhanced rewards构成，谓语动词是will tell，字面翻译是“薪资水平和薪资类型以及奖金发放条件会告诉投资人……”，但这样读起来有点拗口，不如调整语序，以“投资人”为主语构建句子。整句话拟译为：

投资人通过管理人员的薪资水平、薪资类型和奖金发放条件，判断公司是注重短期增长还是长期增长，或者力求在两者之间取得均衡。

（5）You can be certain your investors are looking for insights about what metrics the board uses to assess performance, along with information about incentives and stock ownership levels among managers.

这句话稍微有点复杂，主结构是You can be certain，后面是宾语从句，省略了引导词that，可以按照原文的顺序进行翻译。You can be certain不必对照着译为“你可以肯定”，可以省略“你”，变成汉语的无主句，使得语气表达更加客观。拟译如下：

可以肯定的是，投资人想了解董事会使用何种指标来评估业绩，还想了解管理人员的激励措施和持股水平等相关信息。

3. 合句

前面讲过，英语商务期刊文章有时会使用特别简短的句子，如果相邻的句子都比较简短，或其中一个句子比较简短，而且前后语义连贯，需要考虑合句。

（1）When you meet with investors of any sort, they are likely to ask questions designed to expose your vulnerabilities—operational, financial, and competitive. They will also probe your oversight of the management team.

这里第二句比较简短，其主语they指的就是第一句话主句的主语，所以翻译时要考虑将两句合并，合并之后就可以省略第二句的主语“他们”。拟译如下：

与任何类型的投资人见面，他们都可能会提出一些问题来发现你公司存在的不足，包括经营业绩、财务状况、竞争优势等方面存在的不足，还会探究你如何监管自己的管理团队。

（2）Investors will be curious, too, about the board's operations. They will also ask questions related to social impact.

这两句均比较简短，而且前后两句主语相同，因此要考虑合句。拟译为：

投资人也会对董事会的运作感到好奇，还会问一些与社会影响力有关的问题。

参考译文

与任何类型的投资人见面，他们都可能会提出一些问题来发现你公司存在的不足，包括经营业绩、财务状况、竞争优势等方面存在的不足，还会探究你如何监管自己的管理团队。他们想确认：为提高股东收益（无论是获得短期收益还是长期价值），你在有效管理人才，实施战略，控制风险。

投资人可能还会问你如何为公司和董事会的继任做准备，以及如何确保公司具备持续增长的能力。此外，他们还想知道你如何开发信息资源，以便你对人才市场做出独立判断。管理人员薪资也是经常讨论的话题。投资人通过管理人员的薪资水平、薪资类型和奖金发放条件，判断公司是注重短期增长还是长期增长，或者力求在两者之间取得均衡。例如，年度奖金和报酬往往与股价同步提升，这很正常。但是，如果首席执行官因使股价超过目标价格而获得200%的奖金，这就是注重短期效益的激励方式。如果公司想透支未来资金来实现短期目标，投资人会想知道管理层是否须先征求董事会批准。

投资人也会对董事会的运作感到好奇，还会问一些与社会影响力有关的问题。可以肯定的是，投资人想了解董事会使用何种指标来评估业绩，还想了解管理人员的激励措施和持股水平等相关信息。

第三模块：中文商务期刊语篇英译解析

原文

中国坚持以信息化培育新动能，用新动能推动新发展。以数字经济为代表的新经济蓬勃发展，持续为经济和社会发展注入强劲动力。2020年，中国数字经济总量达到39.2万亿元，占GDP比重达38.6%，同比提升2.4个百分点。电子商务交易额达到37.2万亿元，同比增长4.5%，社交电商异军突起，极大地拓展电子商务发展空间。数字经济领域就业人数达到2.5亿，占2020年总就业人数的26.6%，成为吸纳就业的重要渠道。数字产业化发展迅速，技术应用商业化进程加快，新产业新业态新模式不断涌现。2020年，物联网全年市场规模达到1.67万亿元。网络化协同制造、个性化定制、服务型制造等为传统产业发展带来新亮点。

翻译解析

1. 专业术语

本篇讲的是中国数字经济，涉及经济、电商和互联网等领域，有一些专业术语。这些专业术语的英语表达不难查到，当然也有一些新词汇，需要注意准确翻译。下面列举一些本篇出现的术语和中文特色表达及其英译：

（1）新动能：new drive
（2）数字经济：digital economy
（3）经济总量：economic aggregate
（4）同比：year on year
（5）电子商务：e-commerce
（6）交易额：transaction volume
（7）社交电商：social e-commerce
（8）数字产业化：digital industrialization
（9）物联网：Internet of Things (IoT)
（10）网络化协同制造：coordinative networked manufacturing
（11）个性化定制：personalized customization
（12）服务型制造：service-oriented manufacturing

2. 数字

本篇有不少数字。由于中英文数字的进制不同，中译英时数字有时会译错，所以需要多练习。本篇中的“万亿”和“亿”在翻译时不要译错，例如：

（1） 39.2万亿：39.2 trillion

（2） 2.5亿：250 million

另外，英语中有时会用百分号，但大多数情况下会使用单词 percent 或 per cent来取代百分号。所以本篇中出现的百分数尽量不使用百分号，如38.6%可以写成38.6 percent 或38.6 per cent。

3. 句意的理解与表达

中文句子表达比较灵活，翻译成英语时要注意理解原文的意思；英语更注重形式逻辑，所以中文原文的意思要通过正确的英语形式表达出来。请看本篇中出现的三句话：

（1）中国坚持以信息化培育新动能，用新动能推动新发展。

这句话中的“中国坚持”统领了后面两个部分，译成英文时应该将后面“以信息化培育新动能，用新动能推动新发展”处理为并列成分。整句话拟译为：

China adheres to cultivating the new drive through informatization and promoting new development through the new drive.

（2）以数字经济为代表的新经济蓬勃发展，持续为经济和社会发展注入强劲动力。

这句话首先要厘清主语，理解“持续为经济和社会发展注入强劲动力”的是“新经济”；其次要理解“注入强劲动力”的含义，就是指“促进了……的发展”。翻译时可以将前半句译成主结构，后半句处理为现在分词结构。拟译如下：

New economy represented by digital economy is thriving, boosting economic and social development.

（3）网络化协同制造、个性化定制、服务型制造等为传统产业发展带来新亮点。

这句话中的“带来新亮点”不能直接翻译为bring new highlights。仔细解读原文可以发现，这里的“网络化协同制造、个性化定制、服务型制造”就是“传统产业的新亮点”，所以可以译为：

Coordinative networked manufacturing, personalized customization, and service-oriented manufacturing are new highlights in traditional industries.

4. 并列分句的翻译

本篇中有几个句子由多个并列结构组成，译成英文时要厘清原文的逻辑关系，有时可以翻译成并列结构，有时则需要根据内部逻辑关系转译为英语的主从结构。

（1）2020年，中国数字经济总量达到39.2万亿元，占GDP比重达38.6%，同比提升2.4个百分点。

这句话有多个并列结构，但实际上“占GDP比重达38.6%，同比提升2.4个百分点”补充说明了“中国数字经济总量达到39.2万亿元”，所以这一部分应该变成从属结构，考虑使用现在分词短语和介词短语表示。整句话拟译如下：

In 2020, the digital economic aggregate of the country reached 39.2 trillion *yuan*, accounting for 38.6 percent of the national GDP, with a year-on-year growth of 2.4 percent.

（2）电子商务交易额达到37.2万亿元，同比增长4.5%，社交电商异军突起，极大地拓展电子商务发展空间。

这句话包含了两层意思，前两个小分句是第一层意思，主要讲的是电子商务交易额，之后就是第二层意思。第一层意思中的主结构是“电子商务交易额达到37.2万亿元”，第二层意思中的主结构是“社交电商异军突起”，其余部分可以分别处理为介词短语和现在分词短语形式的从属结构。两部分可以译成两句话，也可以中间用分号隔开。拟译如下：

In the same year, e-commerce transaction volume amounted to 37.2 trillion *yuan*, with a year-on-year growth of 4.5 percent; social e-commerce witnessed rapid development, contributing to the expansion of e-commerce.

（3）数字经济领域就业人数达到2.5亿，占2020年总就业人数的26.6%，成为吸纳就业的重要渠道。

这句话前面讲“数字经济领域就业人数”，后面是“数字经济成为就业渠道”，两部分的主语不一致，所以最好拆分成两句进行翻译。拟译如下：

The number of employees in digital economy was 250 million, accounting for 26.6 percent of the total number of employees that year. Therefore, digital economy is an important field for employment.

（4）数字产业化发展迅速，技术应用商业化进程加快，新产业新业态新模式不断涌现。

这里的三个分句是并列关系，翻译时也可以译成三个并列的主谓结构。拟译如下：

Digital industrialization is developing rapidly, technical application is being commercialized at a high speed, and new industries and new business forms keep emerging.

5. 时态

本篇大部分内容讲的是2020年，这些句子在翻译时要使用过去时，但也有几个句子讲的是现在的一种常态，如第一句和最后一句，可以使用一般现在时。

参考译文

四

China adheres to cultivating the new drive through informatization and promoting new development through the new drive. New economy represented by digital economy is thriving, boosting economic and social development. In 2020, the digital economic aggregate of the country reached 39.2 trillion *yuan*, accounting for 38.6 percent of the national GDP, with a year-on-year growth of 2.4 percent. In the same year, e-commerce transaction volume amounted to 37.2 trillion *yuan*, with a year-on-year growth of 4.5 percent; social e-commerce witnessed rapid development, contributing to the expansion of e-commerce. The number of employees in digital economy was 250 million, accounting for 26.6 percent of the total number of employees that year. Therefore, digital economy is an important field for employment. Digital industrialization is developing rapidly, technical application is being commercialized at a high speed, and new industries and new business forms keep emerging. In 2020, the scale of IoT market was 1.67 trillion *yuan*. Coordinative networked manufacturing, personalized customization, and service-oriented manufacturing are new highlights in traditional industries.

第四模块：翻译练习

1. 英译中

Companies should do what they have promised, even if that doesn't align with an investor's favored strategy. For example, a company has a highly diverse investor base, with widely different timelines for realizing returns. It tries to manage the relationship with each investor but always does what it believes will foster long-term value. The CEO of an insurance company argues for a high degree of openness. He treats stockholders as he would treat co-owners who are siblings, discussing what worries him, what the various businesses are worth, how durable their competitive advantage is, and how he plans to allocate capital. "The CEO absolutely owes that to the owners," he says. "I believe strongly that everybody's entitled to the same information, and that means information about valuation prospects and personnel—exactly what you would tell a silent partner."

Whether to issue earnings guidance is one of the thorniest issues public companies face in dealing with investors. Our advice: Don't do it unless you absolutely have to—and if you do, give yourself plenty of leeway.

2. 中译英

中国持续优化互联网企业发展的市场环境和政策环境，培育了一大批具有创新活力、发展潜力的互联网企业，国际竞争力再上新台阶。截至2021年12月，中国境内外互联网上市企业总数为155家，较2020年增长5.4%，互联网独角兽企业达到219家，千亿级独角兽企业不断涌现，成为推动数字经济发展的闪耀明星。跨境电子商务成为中国电商零售走向国际化的战略，数字经济的快速发展，正在帮助中国更大范围地融入全球经济发展中。

第五单元 旅游

第一模块：旅游翻译概述

旅游文本是一种常见的应用文体，包括景点介绍与宣传、旅游新闻、交通工具介绍、住宿介绍、美食介绍、节日和活动介绍等。不管是英语旅游文本，还是汉语旅游文本，均体现一定的信息性，又体现一定的号召性；既介绍一定的旅游信息，又号召读者采取行动，前往旅游景点。总体说来，英汉旅游文本用词都比较注重宣传性和广告效果，句子比较短小精悍，但也存在一定差异。

一、英文旅游文本的文体特点及其翻译

（一）用词特点

旅游文本也是一种商业宣传文体，英语的宣传文体在提供信息时往往使用一些简单的词汇，使得宣传的内容通俗易懂，为广大读者接受。简单的词汇翻译时也可以平实一点，但总体看来，汉语译文还是要注意美感。另一方面，由于旅游文本在介绍信息的同时旨在宣传景点、酒店、活动、交通等，因此难免会使用渲染词，这些描述性词汇翻译成中文时，不难找到对应的词汇，而且中文的描述性往往更强。

例1

Whether it's winter or summer, or whether you are searching for adventure, fine food or relaxation—the three mountains ensure you'll find what you're looking for.

无论春夏秋冬，无论您渴望冒险、美食还是休闲，这三座山峰都能满足您的心愿。

例2

Camping is an excellent way to experience the country's great outdoors with the added benefit of lots of facilities including swimming pools, restaurants, shops, Wi-Fi, and much more.

体验这个国家不同凡响的户外活动，露营堪称一种不错的选择。游泳池、餐厅、商场、无线网络等诸多设施为游客带来更多便利。

这两个例子的原文用词相对比较简单，翻译时基本直译，但在传达原文信息的基础上，也照顾了汉语读者的审美诉求。

例3

Switzerland has always kept a tight grip on its vibrant, colorful, and quirky traditions. The country's linguistic and cultural diversity and its remote valleys have given rise to a huge and fascinating array of local customs and festivities, many of which still thrive today.

瑞士始终保持其充满活力、多姿多彩、独具特色的传统。这里的语言和文化多种多样，山谷远离尘嚣，孕育了众多迷人的当地风俗和节庆活动，其中有很多风俗和活动至今依然充满旺盛的生命力。

例4

The hotel, featuring 129 stylish rooms and suites, a first-class restaurant, and a stylish bar to linger in, is due to open in spring 2023. The undisputed star attraction will be the top-floor infinity pool, offering breath-taking views of the stunning mountain backdrop.

酒店拥有129个别具风格的客房和套间、一家一流餐厅以及供游客休闲放松的酒吧，预计于2023年春季开业。毫无疑问，位于顶层的无边泳池堪称一颗耀眼的明星，在这里可以欣赏到周围令人叹为观止的群山美景。

例3和例4的英语原文使用了不少形容词，如vibrant、colorful、quirky、fascinating、stylish、breath-taking和stunning，还使用了名词diversity和star attraction。汉语本来就注重描写，所以翻译这些描写性词汇时可以找到对应的甚至更具渲染作用的表达。

英语旅游文本中还常使用第二人称代词you，用于拉近与读者的距离，使读者产生一种亲近感，从而更好地宣传推介产品或服务。翻译时首先考虑是不是可以省译，因为中文有时会使用无主句；如果不能省译，则一般会选用显示礼貌的“您”。请看下面的例子：

五

例5

Instead of joining a guided tour, you can use the map view to go on your own individual city walk or choose one of our suggested routes.

无需导游陪同，就可以利用地图视图在城市里随心漫步，或者选择一条推荐线路游览。

例6

If you prefer another language for the discovery tour through the city, you can download the following audio guide files or rent an audio guide device at the Tourist Information.

如游览这座城市时希望使用其他语言，可以下载以下音频导览文件，或者在游客咨询中心租用音频导览器。

例7

If you like kitsch, you won't want to miss the bizarre melange of cultural artifacts at the National Museum of China.

如果喜欢一般工艺品，（您）一定不想错过中国国家博物馆里各种各样的文化工艺品。

英语旅游文本中经常出现形容词比较级，这些比较级往往暗示最高级，所以一般转译为汉语的最高级，使译文更具说服力，更简洁，也更通顺。

例8

Not a problem at ski-in ski-out hotels, where shifting from sport mode to party mode couldn't be *simpler*.

在可滑雪进出的酒店，这都不是问题，从运动模式转换为派对模式最简单不过了。

例9

There's no *more splendid* way to celebrate the end of the Alps summer.

这堪称庆祝阿尔卑斯夏季结束最精彩的方式。

以上两个例子中，原文使用的比较级实际上暗含了最高级，所以译成汉语的最高级显得更直观，也更具渲染力。

（二）句式特点

旅游文本重点在于推介旅游产品，很多时候需要把更多信息放在一句内阐述清楚，但句子又不能太复杂，因此英语旅游文本中常使用简单句，有些简单句会包含一些短语，例如分词短语、介词短语等。当然，英语旅游文本也会见到简单的复合句。另外，英语旅游文本还经常使用祈使句。请看下面的例子：

例10

An international flock of students and business people stroll along the cobbled streets. Underneath the overhead wires of the electric buses, designers discuss the latest trends of the catwalks of Paris, Milan, and New York. And outside the butcher's shop on the street corner, bankers in suits eat a quick lunch. They inevitably hold a bratwurst in one hand and a crusty roll in the other.

成群结队的国际学生和商务人士沿着鹅卵石街道漫步，电动公共汽车架空线的下面，设计师们讨论着巴黎、米兰和纽约T台上最新的时装。街角的肉铺门口，身着套装的银行工作人员享用着快餐，照例一手拿着德式小香肠，一手拿着脆皮卷。

例11

The environment is friendly. The physical beauty of Hawaii is almost unparalleled. Majestic mountains were created millions of years ago by volcanic activity that thrust these islands three miles from the ocean floor. Wave action across endless eons of time created coral reefs, and then battered and broke them to create miles of white sand beach.

夏威夷环境宜人，美丽的景色无与伦比。数百万年前的火山活动造就了雄伟的高山，形成了这些距离海床高达三英里的岛屿。无休无止的波浪作用形成了珊瑚礁，然后又将珊瑚礁击碎，形成了绵延不绝的白色沙滩。

以上两个例子中，原文基本都是简单句，有些地方使用短语，仅例11的第三句是复合句。翻译简单句时，要注意中文多使用小分句，因此原文的一些句号要改为逗号，使得语义连贯，如例10中的前两句，以及第三、四句都进行了合句处理，中间的句号都改成了逗号。

例12

Enjoy fabulous views of the impressive mountain scenery or historic castles and romantic waterside locations, not forgetting to combine your trip with a

delicious lunch.
欣赏壮丽的群山美景或历史悠久的城堡和浪漫的湖滨区，游览的同时不要忘记享用美味午餐。

例13

Simply select the language you require and load your free copy of the audio city tour onto your PC, then transfer the data onto the electronic device of your choice.
只需选择所需语言，将音频城市导览免费版下载至个人电脑，然后将数据同步到自己选择的电子设备上。

英语旅游文本中的祈使句可以直译，如上面的例12和例13。

（三）修辞特点

旅游文本常使用一些修辞手法，目的是让语言表达更具有吸引力，让读者获得更多的美感，从而激发他们的游览兴趣。英汉两种语言“都有人在不断地研究和改进自己的语言运用艺术，并且逐渐形成了一套特定的表达模式”（李定坤，1994：11），中英文都会使用一些修辞格，因而英语旅游文本中的修辞格基本都可以在汉语中找到对应的表达。

例14

Then came the twilight colors of sea and heaven, the wine pink width of water merging into lawns of aquamarines, the sky *a tender palette* of pink and blue.（比喻）
随之而来的是暮霭沉沉，海天一色，红浪翻涌，碧波横流，天空俨然是柔和的调色板，粉蓝两色交融。

例15

These trains run *every* 20 minutes during the day and *every* hour in the evening until midnight. In the nights from Thursday to Friday, Friday to Saturday and Saturday to Sunday, the shuttle trains run *every* hour all night.（反复）
白天每20分钟有一列火车开行，傍晚至午夜每小时均有一列火车开行。星期四至星期五、星期五至星期六以及星期六至星期日，往返列车每小时一班通宵运行。

例16

Have you heard of Bali, a place to the south of Indonesia? It's a small island but is becoming more and more famous by its fascinating tourist attractions enjoyed by hundreds of thousands of people from world at large.（设问）

您是否听说过印度尼西亚南部的巴厘岛？巴厘岛虽然不大，但迷人的旅游景点越来越受到世界各地游客的青睐，知名度日渐上升。

以上三个例句分别使用比喻、反复和设问的修辞手法，这些句子均可直译。

二、中文旅游文本的文体特点及其翻译

（一）用词特点

中文旅游文本更倾向于使用华丽辞藻和四字格，用以渲染语气，实现感染读者的目的。英语虽然也会在介绍旅游景点或推介旅游项目时使用一些描述性较强的词汇，但总体说来，英语会避免用词重复，通常更简洁。所以，汉语旅游文本中的华丽辞藻和四字格翻译成英文时需要简化。请看下面的例子：

例17

太湖奇峰环抱，烟水迷蒙，自然天成的湖光山色美不胜收。

Surrounded by hills and veiled in mist, the Taihu Lake is a marvelous natural landscape.

例18

江岸上彩楼林立，彩灯高悬，旌旗飘摇，呈现出一派喜气洋洋的节日场面。千姿百态的各式彩龙在江面游弋，舒展着优美的身姿，有的摇头摆尾，风采奕奕；有的喷火吐水，威风八面。

Along the river banks stand tall buildings, ornamented with colored lanterns and bright banners. On the river itself, decorated loong-shaped boats await their challenge, displaying their charms, some wagging their heads and tails and others spraying fire and water.

上述两个例子中，"奇峰环抱""烟水迷蒙""自然天成""湖光山色""美不胜收""彩楼林立""彩灯高悬""旌旗飘摇""喜气洋洋""千姿百态""风

采奕奕”和“威风八面”等四字格都进行了简化处理。另外，请注意，例18中的“龙”没有译成dragon，而是译为loong，以区别于英文dragon的形象。

（二）句式特点

中文旅游文本多用逗号连接若干小分句，读起来充满节奏感。翻译这类句子时，首先找出句子的主要结构，然后将其他小分句转换为附属成分；如果小分句较多，最好设法将之译为短语而非从句，这样使英文句子不至于因为从句太多而显得累赘，符合前文所讲的英文句式特点。当然，小分句如果太多，翻译时也可以考虑拆句处理。

例19

南京属北亚热带季风气候，气候温和，四季分明，冬冷夏热，雨量充沛，光照充足，热量丰富。

Nanjing has a northern subtropical monsoon climate with four distinctive seasons, sufficient rainfall and sunlight, cold in the winter and hot in the summer.

例20

无锡地处长江三角洲，自古物产丰富，是中国著名的“鱼米之乡”。

With abundant resources, Wuxi is a rich city in the Yangtze River Delta, renowned as “land of fish and rice” in China.

中文旅游文本中常用无主句暗示所宣传的旅游项目适合所有读者，有时也是一种无形的建议。由于旅游文本是一种信息兼号召类文体，所以无主句大多数情况下译成英语主动语态的句子，不少情况下需要增加第二人称代词you，这样可以拉近与读者的距离。请看下面的例子：

例21

步入岛中，仿佛置身人间仙境。

On the islet, you will feel as if you were in a fairyland.

例22

如参加观光团，则可在日间畅游著名景点后，于傍晚入座观众席欣赏汇演。

If you are a member of the sight-seeing group, you can take the reserved seat and watch the show in the evening after a day’s visit to famous scenic spots.

前文提到，旅游文本具有号召功能，因此，使用一些祈使句就不足为奇了。汉语旅游文本中的祈使句均可以直译，因为前文说过，英语旅游文本中也会使用祈使句。请看例子：

例23

赶快计划您的新春之旅，以一身喜庆红衣与全港市民一起开心度岁，投入这个欢乐派对吧！

Please lose no time in planning your new-year travel. Spend your Spring Festival with the Hong Kong people in your holiday best. Join this merry party!

例24

花一个下午品尝当地名酒，了解全世界最南端产酒地的奥秘。

Spend one afternoon tasting the local wine and explore the mystery of the wine-producing area at the most southern end of the world.

汉语旅游文本中多使用“名词（话题）+形容词（评述）”的句子或者“名词+名词+形容词”的句子，主要用于对景点进行描述，其中形容词起到了非常重要的描述和渲染作用。这类句子可称作话题–评述句，很多时候不能简单地译成英语的“主语+be+形容词”结构，而应该根据句子的具体情况选择适当的谓语动词。请看下面的例子：

例25

三峡人家风景区，地貌景观丰富，峡谷幽深，树木苍郁，群峰俊秀，清净宜人。

The Tribe of the Three Gorges has/boasts a diversity of landscapes, including valleys, trees, and peaks, which form a quiet and pleasant ambience.

例26

扬州历史悠久，人文荟萃，环境优美，景色秀丽。

Yangzhou is a beautiful city, famous for talented people in its long history.

以上两个例子属于典型的“名词+名词+形容词”结构，没有动词，属于话题–评述句，翻译时根据原文的意思找到主句和附属成分，转译为英语的主谓结构。当然，旅游文本中也有其他形式的话题–评述结构，请看下面的例子：

五

例27

上海的城市交通系统非常发达。公共汽车线路的数量有1500多条，营运车辆1.8万多辆，日均客运量约1398万人次。

Shanghai enjoys a developed urban transportation network, with over 1,500 bus lines made up of 18,000 buses transporting about 13.98 million passengers every day.

例27中第一句跟前面所讲的结构一样，第二句的评述部分则为数量词，这也是汉语中常见的现象。翻译时可以将两部分合句，第一部分成为主句，后面变成短语，结构符合英语的特点。

（三）修辞特点

中文更重审美和渲染，旅游材料中多使用修辞手法。其中，比喻、拟人等常用的修辞大多可以直译，但有时因为文化差异，也只能简化处理。另外，中文更会使用反复、排比、对仗、夸张、用典等修辞手法来表现所宣传景点的美以及悠久的历史与文化。下面来看具体的修辞手法及其翻译。

例28

万里长城是世界闻名的奇迹之一，像一条巨龙盘踞在中国北方的辽阔土地上。它是中国古代劳动人民血汗的结晶，是中国古代文化的象征和中华民族的骄傲。

The Great Wall, one of the wonders of the world, winds its way in vast north China. It came into being thanks to the constructors' hard work. It is one of the symbols of ancient Chinese culture and the Chinese people are proud of it.

例29

长沙这座从远古走到现代的湖湘首邑，虽然历经数千年的风雨沧桑，仍不失古朴美丽的都市风采。

Now Changsha, the capital city of Hunan Province, maintains its unsophisticated beauty with a long history.

例28中“像一条巨龙”和“结晶”都是比喻，这里均省译。例29原文使用了拟人的修辞手法，如“从远古走到现代”“历经沧桑”和“不失风采”，这些拟人手法不宜直接译成英语，因此选择变通处理。

例30

成都，天府之国的都城，南方丝绸之路的起点，你有数千年的文化底蕴，你有千里的肥田沃土，你有千秋名人贤士。

Chengdu, an ancient city lying on the Land of Abundance and the starting point of the Southern Silk Road, boasts vast fertile land and thousands of years' culture created by sages and elites.

该例原文主要使用了排比的修辞手法，即“你有数千年的文化底蕴，你有千里的肥田沃土，你有千秋名人贤士”，当然也有拟人的手法，仿佛与成都对话。原文是主谓结构的排比句，如果在英语中直译，不符合英语的特点，所以选择变通处理，拟人手法也进行了变通处理。整体上只翻译意思，句式结构遵循英语的表达习惯。

例31

洞庭湖“衔远山，吞长江，浩浩汤汤，横无际涯，朝晖夕阴，气象万千”。

The Dongting Lake, vast and mighty, stretches afar, brilliant in the morning and gloomy at dusk.

该例引用范仲淹的《岳阳楼记》，来显示洞庭湖的美及其蕴含的文化，而且还属于夸张手法。如果直接翻译，特别是将“衔远山，吞长江”译成carrying the shadows of distant mountains in it and swallowing the Yangtze River，会让英语读者感到不解，因此需要简化，只译出意思即可。

例32

凤凰古城自然资源丰富，山、水、洞风光无限。山形千姿百态，流瀑万丈垂纱。这里的山不高而秀丽，水不深而澄清，峰岭相摩、河溪萦回，碧绿的江水从古老的城墙下蜿蜒而过，翠绿的南华山麓倒映江心。江中渔舟游船数点，山间暮鼓晨钟兼鸣，河畔上的吊脚楼轻烟袅袅，可谓天人合一。

Fenghuang Town boasts abundant natural resources and fascinating scenery. Here, you can see caves and waterfalls. Magnificent mountains and clear water wind their way around the city. On the water fishing boats come and go, and in the mountains the bell tolls for morning and evening. From the suspended buildings rises faint cooking smoke. Everything is in harmony.

该例原文使用了对仗的修辞手法，包括“山不高而秀丽，水不深而澄清”“江中渔舟游船数点，山间暮鼓晨钟兼鸣”等，其他部分也都极尽渲染之能事。这些对仗和描写如果直译，会显得冗余，因此需要进行简化处理，基本传达出原文的实质信息，适当选择英语中一些描述性的名词短语、形容词和动词等，如boast、abundant、fascinating、wind their way、come and go、toll等。当然，On the water fishing boats come and go, and in the mountains the bell tolls for morning and evening这一句也算适当保留了一点对仗。

总之，中文旅游文本中的修辞手法翻译时要谨慎处理，由于中英文的差异，大多数情况下不能生硬地照搬到英语中去，而应该简化或者变通。

三、旅游文本翻译原则与策略归纳

通过前面的举例分析，我们可以归纳出旅游文本翻译的原则。英语旅游文本翻译成汉语时，措辞要符合汉语读者的审美诉求，因此要注意适当增添美感，修辞也可以直译，句式结构注意使用小分句，用逗号隔开。汉语旅游文本英译时，注意措辞需要低调处理，因此一些修辞格需要简化，句子要注意尽量简单。具体策略可以用下表归纳：

英译中

	英文旅游文本的文体特点	翻译策略
词汇	用词简单	翻译时也可以平实一点，仍然要注意美感。
	渲染词	找到对应的词汇，辞藻甚至更华丽。
	第二人称代词you	省译，不能省译时译成“您”。
	形容词比较级	一般转译为汉语的最高级，使得译文更具说服力，更简洁，更通顺。
句式	简单句	要注意中文多使用小分句，因此可以进行合句处理，使得语义连贯。
	祈使句	直译
修辞	比喻、拟人、反复等	基本都可以直译。

中译英

	中文旅游文本的文体特点	翻译策略
词汇	渲染词、四字格	简化，低调处理。
句式	小分句	译成带有短语的英语简单句，有时需要拆句。
	无主句	添加第二人称代词you做主语，这样可以拉近与读者的距离，有时也可以译成被动语态。
	话题－评述句	找到原文中真正的主谓结构。

（待续）

（续表）

	中文旅游文本的文体特点	翻译策略
修辞	比喻、拟人、反复	大多直译，少部分可简化。
	夸张、排比、对仗、用典	大多简化处理。

第二模块：英文旅游语篇汉译解析

原文

Are you too old for fairy tales? If you think so, Copenhagen is sure to change your mind.

See the city first from the water. In the harbor sits Denmark's best-known landmark: the Little Mermaid. Remember her? She left the world of the Sea People in search of a human soul in one of Hans Christian Andersen's beloved fantasies. From the harbor you can get a feel for the attractive "city of green spires." At twilight or in cloudy weather, the copper-covered spires of old castles and churches lend the city a dream-like atmosphere. You'll think you've stepped into a watercolor painting.

Copenhagen is a city on a human scale. You don't have to hurry to walk the city's center in less than an hour. Exploring it will take much longer. But that's easy. Copenhagen was the first city to declare a street for pedestrians only. The city has less traffic noise and pollution than any other European capital.

Stroll away from the harbor along the riverbanks, you'll see the modest Amalienborg Palace first. Completed in the mid-18th century, it still houses the royal family. The Danish Royal Guard is on duty. At noon, you'll watch the changing of the guard. The guards are not just for show, however. Danes will always remember their heroism on April 9, 1940. When the Nazis invaded Denmark, the guards aimed their guns and fired. The guards would all have been killed if the king hadn't ordered them to surrender.

Copenhagen became the capital of Denmark in 1445. During the late 16th century, trade grew, and so did the city. But fires in 1728 and 1795 destroyed the old wooden structures. Much of what we see today dates from the 19th and early 20th centuries.

翻译解析

1. 专有名词

旅游文本中难免会出现专有名词，一般情况下，翻译时需要查阅网络或相关资料找到中文中已有的固定译法。个别专有名词（包括地名和人名）可能没有固定译文，就需要音译或意译。本篇中出现的几个专有名词都能找到固定译法：

（1） Copenhagen：哥本哈根（丹麦的首都）

（2） the Little Mermaid：小美人鱼（安徒生童话《海的女儿》主人公）

（3） Hans Christian Andersen：安徒生（丹麦童话作家）

（4） Amalienborg Palace：阿美琳堡皇宫（丹麦王宫）

2. 第二人称代词you

一般情况下，旅游文本中的第二人称you均表示泛指，用于拉近与读者的距离。大多数情况下，you需要省译，不能省译时译成中文中的尊称“您”。本篇有几处这样的例子：

（1）Are you too old for fairy tales? If you think so, Copenhagen is sure to change your mind.

第一句中的you显然无法省译，所以就译成“您”。第二句中的条件句在译文中会紧跟前面一句，因此you完全可以省译。整个部分可译为：

您是否已经到了不喜欢童话的年龄？如果真这么认为，哥本哈根一定能够改变您的想法。

（2）You don't have to hurry to walk the city's center in less than an hour.

这句话中的you试着省译后，会发现非常通顺。拟译为：

无需在一小时内匆匆将市中心走完。

3. 措辞

本篇属于典型的英语旅游文本，用词和句子结构均比较简单，措辞比较口语化。但是作为旅游宣传，译文需要迎合中国读者的审美诉求，因此要注意措辞上的美感。比如：

（1） At twilight or in cloudy weather, the copper-covered spires of old castles and churches lend the city a dream-like atmosphere. You'll think you've stepped into a watercolor painting.

这里的twilight可译为“黄昏时分”，cloudy weather为了与“黄昏时分”对应，可译为“阴天之时”。step into可译为“步入”。整句话拟译为：

黄昏时分或阴天之时，古堡和教堂的镀铜塔尖给整个城市增添了梦幻般的气息，会让您感到仿佛步入了一幅水彩画。

（2）Stroll away from the harbor along the riverbanks, you'll see the modest Amalienborg Palace first.

这里stroll可选择“漫步”一词，modest译成“风格朴实的”，you'll see最好不要译成“会看见”，可使用“映入眼帘”这样具有美感的表达。整句话拟译为：

离开港口，沿着河岸漫步，最先映入眼帘的是风格朴实的阿美琳堡皇宫。

4. 一般疑问句

英语旅游文本中经常会使用一般疑问句来激发读者兴趣，大多属于设问，也是在拉近与读者的距离。这样的一般疑问句最好不要直译为“……吗”，而要译成：“您是否……”。比如：

（1）Are you too old for fairy tales?

这句话不建议译成“你已经老得不喜欢童话了吗”，而是译成“您是否已经到了不喜欢童话的年龄”，表达更加通顺。

（2）Remember her?

这句简单的一般疑问句不要译成“还记得她吗”，而建议译成“您是否还记得她”。

5. 合句

英语旅游文本常使用简单句，这些句子不宜直接处理为独立的中文单句。中文文本一般只有意思相对完整才会出现句号，大多数情况下会使用逗号连接一些小分句。因此，旅游文本中的简单句，特别是简短的简单句，在中译文中一般会考虑合句。本篇中有很多简短的句子，翻译时建议考虑合句。比如：

（1）You don't have to hurry to walk the city's center in less than an hour. Exploring it will take much longer. But that's easy.

这里有三个并列单句，前后语义密切相关，因此需要合句。拟译为：

无需在一小时内匆匆将市中心走完，游览这个城市要花上更长的时间，但十分轻松。

（2）Copenhagen was the first city to declare a street for pedestrians only. The city has less traffic noise and pollution than any other European capital.

这里的两个句子都是讲哥本哈根的环保意识，前后意思相连，因此需要合句。拟译为：

哥本哈根是第一个划出步行街的城市，与欧洲其他国家的首都相比，这里的交通噪音和污染少了许多。

（3）Completed in the mid-18th century, it still houses the royal family. The Danish Royal Guard is on duty. At noon, you'll watch the changing of the guard. The guards are not just for show, however.

这里有四个句子，都是在讲阿美琳堡皇宫，意思相连，因此要合句。拟译为：

阿美琳堡皇宫于18世纪中期完工，皇室家族至今居住于此，皇家卫队仍在这里执行任务，中午可以观看卫兵换岗仪式，但他们绝不仅仅是装装样子。

五

参考译文

您是否已经到了不喜欢童话的年龄？如果真这么认为，哥本哈根一定能够改变您的想法。

要看这座城市，先从水看起。丹麦最有名的标志性雕塑小美人鱼就坐落在港口处。您是否还记得她？在安徒生的童话故事里，小美人鱼离开了海底世界，想变成真正的人。安徒生的许多童话故事都颇受青睐。从港口可以领略到哥本哈根这座迷人的“绿色塔尖之城”的魅力。黄昏时分或阴天之时，古堡和教堂的镀铜塔尖给整个城市增添了梦幻般的气息，会让您感到仿佛步入了一幅水彩画。

哥本哈根是很人性化的城市。无需在一小时内匆匆将市中心走完，游览这个城市要花上更长的时间，但十分轻松。哥本哈根是第一个划出步行街的城市，与欧洲其他国家的首都相比，这里的交通噪音和污染少了许多。

离开港口，沿着河岸漫步，最先映入眼帘的是风格朴实的阿美琳堡皇宫。阿美琳堡皇宫于18世纪中期完工，皇室家族至今居住于此，皇家卫队仍在这里执行任务，中午可以观看卫兵换岗仪式，但他们绝不仅仅是装装样子。丹麦人永远记得他们在1940年4月9日的英勇事迹。当时纳粹分子入侵丹麦，卫兵举枪瞄准并且开火。如果国王不叫他们投降的话，这些卫兵可能都已战死沙场。

哥本哈根于1445年成为丹麦的首都。16世纪末，贸易发展带动了城市的发展。但是，城中的旧式木建筑在1728年和1795年的两场大火中烧毁，今天我们看到的大部分建筑都建于19世纪和20世纪初。

第三模块：中文旅游语篇英译解析

原文

北京位于华北平原西北边缘，背靠燕山山脉，是中国的政治和文化中心，也是世界著名的古都和现代化国际大都市。

北京是世界上拥有世界遗产最多的城市，七处分别是故宫、天坛、颐和园、明十三陵、长城、周口店北京人遗址、京杭大运河。北京曾为五代都城，拥有丰富的皇家建筑和浓郁的传统文化。故宫完美体现了中国传统的古典风格；天坛以其布局合理、构筑精妙而扬名中外；明十三陵是北京最大的皇家陵寝墓群；绵延万里的长城是人间建筑奇迹。幽深的胡同、亲切的四合院、铿锵的京剧……弥漫于宫阙和胡同的浓浓京味使人沉迷。

北京还是一座现代化的国际大都市，高楼大厦鳞次栉比，王府井步行街霓虹闪烁，中关村飞速发展，中央商务区是北京繁华的象征，“鸟巢”成了新北京的现代符号。

北京的文化生活丰富多彩，各种类型的演出、展会等一应俱全。北京是世界级的“美食之城”，风味小吃历史悠久、品种繁多，世界各地的风味美食也都能在北京找到吃处。

翻译解析

1. 专有名词

中文旅游文本中难免出现中国的地名和景点名。其中地名一般使用音译，景点名称要查阅网站，确认是否已有固定译法，如果有，就需要沿用固定译名；如果没有，则根据具体情况判断是音译还是意译。本篇出现的专有名词中，地名均使用汉语拼音，景点名均已有固定译法。

（1）华北平原：the North China Plain

（2）燕山山脉：the Yanshan Mountains

（3）故宫：the Forbidden City

（4）天坛：the Temple of Heaven

（5）颐和园：the Summer Palace

（6）明十三陵：the Ming Tombs

（7）长城：the Great Wall

（8）周口店北京人遗址：the Peking Man Site at Zhoukoudian

（9）京杭大运河：the Grand Canal

（10）京剧：Beijing Opera

（11）王府井步行街：Wangfujing Pedestrian Street

（12）中关村：Zhongguancun

（13）“鸟巢”：the Bird’s Nest

需要注意的是，像“燕山山脉”这样的专有名词中，名称只有一个“燕”字，一般需要音译为两个字的汉语拼音，即 the Yanshan Mountains。有一些中国特色的普通名词现在也倾向先使用音译，再在括号内进行解释，如本篇中出现的“胡同”和“四合院”，分别译为*hutong* (lane) 和 *siheyuan* (four-section compound)，无需大写，但需要用斜体表示。

2. 渲染词

前文讲到，由于中文往往重艺术和审美效果，汉语旅游文本中经常出现一些描写意味非常浓厚的词语或表达，有的具有浓重的渲染色彩。鉴于英汉两种语言的区别，翻译这些表达时需要低调处理。请看本篇中出现的几个例子：

（1）天坛以其布局合理、构筑精妙而扬名中外；明十三陵是北京最大的皇家陵寝墓群；绵延万里的长城是人间建筑奇迹。

这里的“布局合理、构筑精妙”属于渲染词汇，翻译时无需一一对应；“绵延万里”也无需翻译成extend tens of thousands of miles。整句话可译为：

The Temple of Heaven is famous for its layout, the Ming Tombs are the largest imperial tomb complex in Beijing, and the Great Wall is a construction wonder of the world.

（2）幽深的胡同、亲切的四合院、铿锵的京剧……弥漫于宫阙和胡同的浓浓京味使人沉迷。

这里的“幽深”“亲切”“铿锵”以及“弥漫于宫阙和胡同的浓浓京味使人沉迷”均需要简化，否则译文会显得比较冗余，让英语读者感觉拗口或难以理解。整句话可译为：

Beijing is also famous for its *hutong* (lane), *siheyuan* (four-section compound), and Beijing Opera.

（3）北京的文化生活丰富多彩，各种类型的演出、展会等一应俱全。

这里的“丰富多彩”“一应俱全”实际上与“各种类型”同义，因此可以合并为英语中常用的一个短语a diversity of。整句话拟译为：

The city has a diversity of cultural offers, including performances and exhibitions.

3. 汉语并列结构转译为英语主从结构

汉语倾向使用并列小分句，英语则更倾向使用主从结构，而且旅游文本的句子不能过于复杂，因此，汉语文本中的并列小分句在转译为英语主从结构时，还要注意从属结构最好使用一些短语而非从句。请看下面几例：

（1）北京位于华北平原西北边缘，背靠燕山山脉，是中国的政治和文化中心，也是世界著名的古都和现代化国际大都市。

该句由四个小分句组成，可以先找出主语是“北京”，其主要谓语为“是中国的……，也是世界……”，这两小句可以并列，前面的“位于……”和“背靠……”要考虑使用短语做从属部分，如状语或后置定语。拟译如下：

Located on the northwestern edge of the North China Plain, Beijing, with the Yanshan Mountains to its north, is the political and cultural center of the country and a world-renowned ancient capital city and modern cosmopolitan.

（2）北京是世界上拥有世界遗产最多的城市，七处分别是故宫、天坛、颐和园、明十三陵、长城、周口店北京人遗址、京杭大运河。

这一句由两个小分句组成，后面的部分就是在列举前文提到的“世界遗产”，所以这句话很容易转换成英语的主从结构，将后面的部分译为“世界遗产”的同位语即可。拟译如下：

Beijing has the most UNESCO World Heritage Sites across the globe, namely, the Forbidden City, the Temple of Heaven, the Summer Palace, the Ming Tombs, the Great Wall, the Peking Man Site at Zhoukoudian, and the Grand Canal.

（3）北京是世界级的“美食之城”，风味小吃历史悠久、品种繁多，世界各地的风味美食也都能在北京找到吃处。

这一句由三个并列结构组成，但语义重心是第一部分，后面两个部分都是对“美食之城”的补充说明，可考虑用短语结构进行翻译。拟译为：

It is a world-famous city for gourmets, with varieties of traditional food of Chinese and exotic flavor.

4. 拆句

汉语因为并列结构多，又属于意合语言，所以有的句子逗号很多，整个句子比较长，有时为照顾到英语旅游文本句子简短的特点，需要做拆句处理。本篇中的例子如下：

北京还是一座现代化的国际大都市，高楼大厦鳞次栉比，王府井步行街霓虹闪烁，中关村飞速发展，中央商务区是北京繁华的象征，“鸟巢”成了新北京的现代符号。

这句话由六个小分句组成，前面两个分句表述的内容更宽泛，后面四个分句列举具体地方的情况。如果翻译成一句英文，即使使用一些短语，也会显得冗长，不符合英语旅游文本句式结构的特点。因此，考虑拆句，先从

“鳞次栉比”断开，后面的部分也可译成简短的英语句子。需要注意的是，最后两个分句的谓语动词都是is，因此可以合在一起，后一并列分句省略谓语动词is。整句话拟译为：

It is also a modern cosmopolitan, home to numerous skyscrapers. The Wangfujing Pedestrian Street is crowded day and night. The Zhongguancun develops rapidly. The CBD is the symbol of prosperity in China, and the Bird's Nest, the icon of modern Beijing.

另外，本篇翻译还要注意适当使用代词。原文中多次重复“北京”，但英语更注重替代，因此有些地方需要用代词it或者上义词city来替代Beijing。具体可参阅下面的参考译文。

参考译文

Located on the northwestern edge of the North China Plain, Beijing, with the Yanshan Mountains to its north, is the political and cultural center of the country and a world-renowned ancient capital city and modern cosmopolitan.

Beijing has the most UNESCO World Heritage Sites across the globe, namely, the Forbidden City, the Temple of Heaven, the Summer Palace, the Ming Tombs, the Great Wall, the Peking Man Site at Zhoukoudian, and the Grand Canal. As the capital of five dynasties in Chinese history, it is home to imperial buildings and a strong traditional atmosphere. The Forbidden City embodies traditional imperial architecture style, the Temple of Heaven is famous for its layout, the Ming Tombs are the largest imperial tomb complex in Beijing, and the Great Wall is a construction wonder of the world. Beijing is also famous for its *hutong* (lane), *siheyuan* (four-section compound), and Beijing Opera.

It is also a modern cosmopolitan, home to numerous skyscrapers. The Wangfujing Pedestrian Street is crowded day and night. The Zhongguancun develops rapidly. The CBD is the symbol of prosperity in China, and the Bird's Nest, the icon of modern Beijing.

The city has a diversity of cultural offers, including performances and exhibitions. It is a world-famous city for gourmets, with varieties of traditional food of Chinese and exotic flavor.

第四模块：翻译练习

1. 英译中

Magical ski regions, perfectly prepared pistes, superb deep-snow slopes—Switzerland offers everything a skier's heart could desire. And the icing on the cake for avid skiers is a hotel located in the middle of the ski area: Ski-in ski-out means you can simply wake up, get up, and hit the slopes.

Located high up in the ski areas themselves, ski-in ski-out hotels provide everything you'll need to enjoy an unforgettable holiday in the snow. Exceptional cuisine and traditional Swiss hospitality will ensure that you feel completely at home in these hotels.

Even a really spectacular day on the slopes has to come to an end sometime. Not a problem at ski-in ski-out hotels, where shifting from sport mode to party mode couldn't be simpler. No matter how long you spend doing a bit of après-ski in the bar or on the dance floor, you know that all you have to do tomorrow is jump out of bed and onto your skis.

2. 中译英

西安城墙和西安碑林，都是闻名中外的历史文化旅游景区。西安城墙景区，是以西安古城墙为主题，集护城河、环城林带、顺城路四位一体的环城风景区，是保存最完整的中国古代城垣建筑。碑林是收藏中国古代碑石时间最早，收藏名碑最多的汉族文化艺术宝库。从南门登上城墙一路往东，从城头即可看到古典庄重的碑林博物馆；站在碑林博物馆门口，抬头就能看到雄伟厚重的西安城墙。西安城墙和西安碑林，二者毗邻而处，相得益彰，已成为游客来到古城西安，不容错过的一张靓丽名片。

第六单元　科技

第一模块：科技翻译概述

“科技”是“科学”和“技术”的合称，顾名思义，科技文本就是以“科学”和“技术”为主题的文本。所以科技文本的翻译就是科学和技术领域各种主题文本的翻译。无论英语科技文本，还是中文科技文本，均属于信息类文本。此类文本旨在传递信息，在文体上都有共同的特点，条理清楚，结构严谨，用词专业，句式符合规范，语气正式、客观。所以，在翻译过程中要做到专业术语规范，句式结构正确，表达清晰，译文语气也要正式、客观。

一、英文科技文本的文体特点及其翻译

（一）用词特点

首先，英语科技文本会使用科技相关领域的专业术语，这些术语一定要查阅相关资料或网站。特别值得注意的是，有些普通词汇在英语科技文本中会有专门的意思，如果不假思索就将其翻译为普通词汇，势必会闹出笑话。

例1

The grinding machine raises the precision of the workpiece and improves its surface *finish*.

磨床可以提高工件的精度与表面的光洁度。

例2

Rejection was discovered in 1940s. When human organs are transferred from person to person, the immune system attacks and destroys what it sees as a *foreign substance*.

20世纪40年代发现了排异反应。器官从一个人移植到另一个人时，受体的免疫系统会将其视为异物进行攻击和破坏。

例3

Aluminum oxide is a black *coating* that is very effective for machining *cast irons* and in other applications.

氧化铝属于黑色涂层，用于各种铸铁加工和其他方面，效果显著。

以上例子中，finish不是大家所熟悉的"完成"之意，rejection不是"抛弃、拒绝"之意，而具有了专业的含义，所以汉语译文要准确。另外，像foreign substance、aluminum oxide、coating、cast iron也都是专业术语，汉语均需使用对应的术语表达。

科技英语中名词化比较明显，特别是由动词和形容词加后缀变来的名词使用频繁。这也是英语信息类文本的共同特点。翻译此类名词时大多转译为动词或形容词。请看下面的例子：

例4

Shaking and ground *displacement* often causes the severing of electrical and gas lines leading to the *development* of many localized fires.

晃动和地面位移往往引起电线和燃气管线裂开，从而会发生许多局部火灾。

例5

Prefabrication is by no means a new idea, but in the past, unimaginative *uniformity* in design, together with limited materials, led to a natural *distaste* for this form of construction.

建筑构件预制不是新概念，但是在过去，设计缺乏想象，形式单一，而且材料有限，使得该种建筑方式不受青睐。

例6

The *violation* of parity conservation would lead to an electric dipole moment for all systems.

破坏宇称守恒会导致所有系统产生一个电偶极矩。

（二）句式特点

英语科技文本的句子一般比较长，句子层次比普通文体中的句子要复杂一些，翻译前需要对句子结构进行分析，先找主结构，再找次要结构，逻辑理清之后再进行翻译，这样才能保证准确传达原文的意思。请看下面的例子：

例7

A wide range of materials for use in medicine, agriculture, and industry that are currently in short supply could be produced in much greater quantities if the genes regulating their production by higher plants and animal cells could be incorporated into the microbial genome.

用于医学、农业和工业的许多材料目前十分紧缺，但某些基因可通过高等植物和动物细胞来影响这些材料生产，如果将这些基因导入微生物基因组，材料的产量便可大幅度提高。

这句话的主结构是A wide range of materials ... could be produced，之后是一个条件状语从句，主结构里面的materials跟了两个定语，一个是介词短语for use ...，一个是定语从句that are currently ...。厘清了这些关系再进行翻译就简单多了。需要注意的是，为了符合汉语的特点，译文可以使用一些小分句。

例8

Bio-industry is reorganizing itself to respond to these trends: Conscious of the economic stakes involved in the enormous potential markets for the new biotechnological products, many chemical, pharmaceutical, petrochemical, and industrial food corporations are creating their own research laboratories in plant biology and physiology and are investing in small venture capital companies engaged in advance research as well as in larger companies with R&D experience.

生物工业正在重组以应对这些趋势：化工、制药、石化和工业食品等领域的许多企业已经意识到新生物技术产品巨大的潜在市场中有着丰厚的经济利益，所以正在兴建自己的植物生物学和生理学研究实验室，并投资从事前沿研究的小型风险资本公司和拥有研发经验的大型公司。

这个句子冒号前后是两句话，前面比较简单，后面的主结构是many chemical, pharmaceutical, petrochemical, and industrial food corporations are creating ... and are investing ...，然后再把其他成分分析出来即可。也要注意汉

语译文应使用一些分句。

科技英语中一个显著的句法特点就是被动语态使用比较频繁。之所以使用被动语态，是因为科技文本一般都注重客观科学。但是，由于汉语中被动语态使用较少，因此大多数情况下，科技英语文本中的被动句要转译为汉语的主动句。请看下面的例子：

例9

This procedure is key, because once the phonemes can be located and labeled, the software can precisely catalogue them for use in a searchable database.

该程序属于关键程序，因为一旦能辨识并标出音素，软件便能对音素进行精确分类，建立可供搜索的数据库，以备日后使用。

例10

The ancient Chinese sages said that illness and disease should first be treated with diet, then acupuncture and then Chinese herbs.

中国古代圣人认为，疾病应该首先通过饮食进行治疗，其次是针灸，再其次是草药。

以上两个例子中的被动语态如果将“被”字译出，读起来会很拗口，转译为主动语态更符合汉语的表达习惯。当然，有些被动语态也会在译文中保留，特别是对于动作的承受者来说，后面动词所代表的动作如果对这个承受者是不好的事情，可以使用“被”“遭”“受”等被动语态标识。例如：

例11

If a lower life form is killed, other species that depend on it will also be affected.

如果低等生命形式遭到破坏，依赖于该生命形式的其他物种也会受到影响。

例12

Both natural vegetation and crops are affected by acid rain. The roots are damaged by acidic rainfall, causing the growth of the plant to be stunted, or even its death.

自然植被和庄稼都受到酸雨的影响。其根部遭到酸雨的破坏，使得植物的生长受到阻碍，甚至引起植物死亡。

以上两个例子中，被动语态的动词对动作的承受者来说是负面的，所以翻译时可以译成汉语的被动语态，使用了“遭到”“受到”等汉语被动语态的标志词。

二、中文科技文本的文体特点及其翻译

（一）用词特点

中文科技文本存在一些专业词汇，这些词汇翻译时要在英语中找到对应的表达方式，不能随便翻译。请看下面的例子：

例13

光伏发电是根据光生伏特效应原理，利用太阳能电池将太阳光能直接转化为电能。

Photovoltaic power generation is based on the principle of photovoltaic effect. The energy is directly converted from the sunlight into electrical energy through solar cells.

例14

随着中国互联网产业的不断壮大，数据中心从小规模简单存储计算中心转向以支持网络信息服务为核心的互联网数据中心，功能从简单的“数据仓库”发展成为集数据交互、信息处理和数据分析于一体的综合服务。

With the development of China's Internet industry, data centers are developing from small simple storage and computing ones to *Internet Data Centers (IDCs)* that can support network information services. They have evolved from simple “data warehouses” into centers providing comprehensive services including data exchange, information processing, and data analysis.

例15

网络钓鱼是社会工程学欺骗原理与网络技术相结合的典型应用，是通过构造与某一目标网站高度相似的页面诱骗用户的攻击方式。

Phishing is the typical application of the combination between social engineering deception and network technology. In this attack, a website similar with the targeted one is constructed to trick the users.

以上三个例子中，“光伏发电”“光生伏特效应”“互联网数据中心”“数据仓库”“数据交互”“网络钓鱼”均属于专业性较强的词语，翻译时要注意

找到英语的对应表达。

中文科技文本中有些句子使用动词比较多，翻译时需要根据具体情况进行判断，如果有些动词在英语译文中不处理为谓语动词，而可能是主语或宾语成分时，要考虑将这些动词转译成名词形式。请看下面的例子：

例16

电视模拟信号改成了数字信号，使图像更加清晰真切。

The *change* of simulated signals into digital signals makes TV pictures much clearer and more vivid.

例17

自动化要求不断详细了解机器系统的操作，以便一旦有必要就立即采取最佳校正措施。

Automation involves a detailed and continuous *knowledge* of the operation of the machine system, so that the best corrective actions can be taken immediately when necessary.

例16中“改成……”实际上可以作为“使图像更加清晰真切”的主语，所以将其英译为名词。例17中“了解……”是“要求”的宾语，译文也转译为名词，这样表述更加客观，也符合英语静态化的语言特点。

（二）句式特点

中文科技文本中的句子一般比较长，其中的小分句也相对较长，翻译时要先进行分析，厘清逻辑关系。

例18

超级计算机具有很强的计算和处理数据的能力，主要特点表现为高速度和大容量，配有多种外部和外围设备及丰富的高功能软件系统。

The supercomputer has super capability of computing and processing data, characterized by high speed and large capacity, and equipped with many external and peripheral devices and high-performance software systems.

翻译这句话时，先找出在英语句子中可以做主结构的部分，然后看其他部分是否可以用短语或从句来做次要结构。仔细阅读原文发现，可将第一个分句“超级计算机具有很强的计算和处理数据的能力”作为主结构，后面的“主要特点……”“配有……”可以分别用characterized by和equipped with加名词的形式进行翻译，这样整个句子的翻译就迎刃而解了。

例19

气体传感器是指将被检测的气体分子与气敏材料发生的物理或化学反应所产生的物理或化学量变化，转变为可有效测量的电信号、光信号、声信号等，从而对气体种类和浓度进行测量的一种传感器。

A gas sensor is a sensor that transforms the detected physical or chemical quantity change generated by a physical or chemical reaction between gas molecules and gas sensitive materials into effectively measurable electrical, optical or acoustical signals for the measurement of gas type and concentration.

这句话确实比较长，要细细解读。通过分析会发现，该句实际上是在给“气体传感器”下定义，即“气体传感器是……一种传感器”，因此，这句话的主结构就提炼出来了，剩余的部分均为“一种传感器”的定语。定语部分的主要意思是“为实现对……测量，将物理或化学量变化转变为……信号”。经过这样的解读，英语译文也就基本出来了。

中文科技文本中常使用无主句，因为无主句无需说出动作的发出者，显得客观、科学。

例20

把油加入水中，会在水面形成一层油膜，使得空气隔绝，水中的含氧量会急剧下降。

Addition of oil to water will dramatically reduce the amount of oxygen in the water due to the formation of an oil film on the water surface, which prevents air from entering the water below.

例21

操作前，须对零件进行认真检查，从而保证操作过程能够顺利完成。

Before operation, all parts have to be examined carefully for the success of operation.

以上两个无主句中，例20将抽象名词短语作为主语，显得很客观；例21译为被动语态，也能够保留原文的语气。当然，例21也可以译成抽象名词做主语的主动语态，即：Before operation, a careful examination of all parts can ensure the success of operation.

三、科技文本翻译原则与策略归纳

综上所述，科技文本的翻译原则包括以下几点：（1）准确传达原文信息。科技文本通常都是客观真实的信息，因此翻译时需要忠实准确地传达信息。（2）术语翻译准确到位。中英文科技文本均包含一定的专业术语，翻译时要在目的语中找到对应表达。（3）译文行文清晰。科技文本翻译时要分析出原文的逻辑关系，以免传达错误。（4）语态选择要符合目的语的习惯。例如，英文倾向使用被动语态，翻译成中文时大多要转换成主动语态；中译英时正好相反。

英译中

	英文科技文本的文体特点	翻译策略
词汇	专业术语	翻译成汉语对应的专业术语。
	由动词或形容词派生而来的抽象名词	转译为汉语的动词。
句式	长句	先厘清原文逻辑关系，然后再翻译。
	被动句	一般转译为主动句，有时根据意思可以直译为汉语的被动句。

中译英

	中文科技文本的文体特点	翻译策略
词汇	专业术语	在英语中找到对应表达。
	动词使用比较频繁	转译为英语的名词，显得更加科学和客观。
句式	长句	先对句子进行分析，找到主干结构，然后再分析其他部分；如果找到的主结构不止一个，则拆句处理。
	无主句	译成抽象名词做主语的英语句子或使用被动句。

第二模块：英文科技语篇汉译解析

六

原文

Life, for all its complexities, has a simple commonality: It spreads. Plants, animals, and bacteria have colonized almost every nook and cranny of our world.

Some scientists speculate that biological matter may have proliferated across the cosmos itself, transported from planet to planet on wayward lumps of rock and ice. This idea is known as panspermia, and it carries a profound implication: Life on Earth may not have originated on our planet.

In theory, panspermia is fairly simple. Astronomers know that impacts from comets or asteroids on planets will sometimes eject debris with enough force to catapult rocks into space. Some of those space rocks will, in turn, crash into other worlds. A few rare meteorites on Earth are known to have come from Mars, likely in this fashion.

"You can imagine small astronauts sitting inside this rock, surviving the journey," says Avi Loeb, an astrophysicist at Harvard University and director of the school's Institute for Theory and Computation. "Microbes could potentially move from one planet to another, from Mars to Earth, from Earth to Venus."

Loeb has authored a number of papers probing the mechanics of panspermia, looking at, among other things, how the size and speed of space objects might affect their likelihood of transferring life. While Loeb still thinks it's more likely that life originated on Earth, he says his work has failed to rule out the possibility that it came from somewhere else in space.

If an asteroid or comet is large enough, microbes could be frozen deep within, Loeb says. That could protect them from radiation and the extreme temperatures that turn meteors into fireballs. After asteroids or comets explode onto the surface of a new world, these extraterrestrial colonists could begin to thrive.

翻译解析

本篇的主题是生命的起源问题，属于比较典型的科技文章。里面有一些关于太空的专业表达以及几个专有名词，有些句子比较长，还有些地方使用了被动语态。

1. 专业术语

（1） proliferate：繁殖
（2） panspermia：泛种论/生物外来论
（3） comet：彗星
（4） asteroid：小行星
（5） meteorite：陨石
（6） Mars：火星
（7） astrophysicist：天体物理学家
（8） Venus：金星

2. 专有名词

本篇有一个人名和两个机构名，其中Harvard University是大家熟悉的哈佛大学，其他两个要利用网络资源查阅是否已有中文译名。

（1） Avi Loeb：阿维·罗布
（2） Harvard University：哈佛大学
（3） Institute for Theory and Computation：理论与计算研究所

3. 生动表达

本篇主题是对生命起源的推测，虽然属于科技文本，但有几个表达非常生动，有的是固定短语，有的是拟人手法，值得学习。

（1） every nook and cranny：每个角落
（2） small astronaut：小宇航员（这里将微生物拟人化）
（3） extraterrestrial colonist：地球以外的殖民者（这里也是将微生物拟人化）

4. 长句

本篇写作的风格比较明快，大部分句子长度都适中，只有少数句子偏长，翻译时需要分析结构，厘清逻辑关系。

（1）This idea is known as panspermia, and it carries a profound implication: Life on Earth may not have originated on our planet.

这句话由三个分句组成，属于并列关系，可以按原文的顺序翻译。拟译如下：

这一假说称为“生物外来论”，其中包含着一种意味深长的暗示：地球上的生命可能并非起源于地球。

（2）Loeb has authored a number of papers probing the mechanics of panspermia, looking at, among other things, how the size and speed of space objects might affect their likelihood of transferring life.

这句话的主结构是Loeb has authored a number of papers，后面probing the mechanics of panspermia做后置定语，修饰papers，looking at ...到句末是现在分词做状语，其逻辑主语是Loeb。整句话拟译如下：

罗布撰写了多篇论文探讨“生物外来论”的原理，研究太空物体的大小和速度如何影响其搭载生命的可能性等问题。

（3）While Loeb still thinks it's more likely that life originated on Earth, he says his work has failed to rule out the possibility that it came from somewhere else in space.

这句话前面是while引导的让步状语从句，后面的主句中又有一个that引导的同位语从句，解释说明possibility。整句话拟译为：

尽管罗布依然认为生命起源于地球的可能性更大，但他表示，自己的研究未能排除生命起源于地球之外的可能性。

5. 被动语态

本篇有几个地方使用了被动语态，首先考虑这些被动句式是否可以转译为汉语的主动句，如果不能再根据具体情况译成被动句。

（1）A few rare meteorites on Earth are known to have come from Mars, likely in this fashion.

这里的be known不能直译成“被知道”，可以将被动部分译为“众所周知”。整句话拟译为：

众所周知，地球上存在少数来自火星的罕见陨石，这些陨石很可能就是以上述方式来到地球的。

（2）If an asteroid or comet is large enough, microbes could be frozen deep within, Loeb says.

这句话中被动语态的施动者是an asteroid or comet，可以按照原句顺序翻译，在形式上转译成主动句。另外，建议将Loeb says提到句首，更符合汉语的表达习惯。整句话拟译如下：

罗布认为，如果小行星或彗星足够大，就可能将微生物冷冻在内部。

6. 合句

本篇最后一段的前两句建议合句处理：

If an asteroid or comet is large enough, microbes could be frozen deep within, Loeb says. That could protect them from radiation and the extreme temperatures that turn meteors into fireballs.

第二句中的第一个that指的是前面所说的内容，从语义上看，两句是紧密关联的，所以建议合句。拟译如下：

罗布认为，如果小行星或彗星足够大，就可能将微生物冷冻在内部，这样可以保护微生物免受辐射以及将流星变成火球的极端温度的影响。

参考译文

生命尽管复杂，但有一个简单的共通之处：生命都可以传播。世界的每个角落几乎都有动植物和细菌在大量繁殖。

有些科学家推测，生物可能在宇宙中繁殖，搭乘任意岩块和冰块从一个星球前往另一个星球。这一假说称为“生物外来论”，其中包含着一种意味深长的暗示：地球上的生命可能并非起源于地球。

理论上，“生物外来论”相当简单。天文学家知道，彗星或小行星撞击行星时产生的冲击有时产生碎片，其推力足以将岩石抛入太空。这些进入太空的岩石有些会破碎，闯入其他世界。众所周知，地球上存在少数来自火星的罕见陨石，这些陨石很可能就是以上述方式来到地球的。

“可以想象一些小‘宇航员’就坐在这块岩石中，在漫长的旅途中活了下来。”哈佛大学天体物理学家，理论与计算研究所主任阿维·罗布这样说道，“微生物极有可能从一个星球转移到另一个星球，从火星到地球，从地球到金星。”

罗布撰写了多篇论文探讨“生物外来论”的原理，研究太空物体的大小和速度如何影响其搭载生命的可能性等问题。尽管罗布依然认为生命起源于地球的可能性更大，但他表示，自己的研究未能排除生命起源于地球之外的可能性。

罗布认为，如果小行星或彗星足够大，就可能将微生物冷冻在内部，这样可以保护微生物免受辐射以及将流星变成火球的极端温度的影响。小行星或彗星在新世界表面爆炸后，这些地球以外的“殖民者”就开始茁壮成长。

第三模块：中文科技语篇英译解析

原文

自然语言处理技术是人工智能的一个重要分支，其目的是利用计算机对自然语言进行智能化处理。基础的自然语言处理技术主要围绕语言的不同层级展开，包括音位、形态、词汇、句法、语义、语用、篇章7个层级。这些基本的自然语言处理技术经常运用到下游的多种自然语言处理任务中，如机器翻译、对话、问答、文档摘要等。

科学家研究自然语言处理技术的目的是让机器能够理解人类语言，用自然语言的方式与人类交流，最终拥有“智能”。人工智能时代，我们希望计算机拥有视觉、听觉、语言和行动的能力，其中语言是人类区别于动物的最重要特征之一，语言是人类思维的载体，也是知识凝练和传承的载体。在人工智能领域，研究自然语言处理技术的目的就是让机器理解并生成人类的语言，从而和人类平等流畅地沟通交流。

翻译解析

本篇的主题是人工智能和语言，属于科技文体。里面含有一些人工智能和语言学术语，还有一些长句。

1. 专业术语

（1）自然语言处理技术：natural language processing (NLP)

（2）人工智能：artificial intelligence (AI)

（3）音位：phonology

（4）形态：morphology

（5）词汇：lexicology

（6）句法：syntax

（7）语义：semantics

（8）语用：pragmatics

（9）篇章：discourse

（10）机器翻译：machine translation

2. 被动语态

本篇有的句子形式是主动，实际上意义被动，翻译时要考虑使用被动句。另外，科技文本中一些句子使用泛指主语，如“我们”“人们”等，这些句子最好也译成英语的被动句。

（1）基础的自然语言处理技术主要围绕语言的不同层级展开，包括音位、形态、词汇、句法、语义、语用、篇章7个层级。

这句话中的“自然语言处理技术”和“展开”实际上是被动关系，所以该句可以翻译为被动语态。拟译为：

Basic NLP is done to different hierarchical levels of languages, including phonology, morphology, lexicology, syntax, semantics, pragmatics, and discourse.

（2）这些基本的自然语言处理技术经常运用到下游的多种自然语言处理任务中，如机器翻译、对话、问答、文档摘要等。

这句话中的“自然语言处理技术”和“运用”之间也是被动关系，可以译为被动语态。另外，该句主语和上一句一致，可以用代词避免重复。拟译如下：

It has been applied to multiple natural language processing tasks downstream, including machine translation, dialog, Q&A, and document summarization.

（3）人工智能时代，我们希望计算机拥有视觉、听觉、语言和行动的能力。

这句话的主语是“我们”，属于泛指主语，所以也建议翻译成被动语态，凸显科技文本的客观性。拟译如下：

In the era of AI, the computer is expected to have the ability to see, hear, speak, and act.

3. 长句

本篇有几个句子稍长，翻译前建议先对句子进行分析，看能否找到一个主结构，其他变成次要结构，这样就可以译为英语简单句。如果分析时发现，主结构不止一个，就需要拆分成两个或两个以上的英语句子。

（1）自然语言处理技术是人工智能的一个重要分支，其目的是利用计算机对自然语言进行智能化处理。

这句话前半部分是主结构，后半部分是目的状语，可以用过去分词短语表示。拟译为：

Natural language processing (NLP) is a branch of artificial intelligence (AI), aimed for intelligent processing of natural languages with the computer.

（2）人工智能时代，我们希望计算机拥有视觉、听觉、语言和行动的能力，其中语言是人类区别于动物的最重要特征之一，语言是人类思维的载体，也是知识凝练和传承的载体。

这句话比较长，其中包含多个分句。分析句意后会发现，该句可大致分为两个部分，“人工智能时代，我们希望计算机拥有……的能力”具有一定概括性，后面的部分着重讲其中的“语言能力”，因此可以从这里断开。第二部分也包含很多内容，还需进一步拆分。整个句子考虑拆译为三个句子，拟译如下：

In the era of AI, the computer is expected to have the ability to see, hear, speak, and act. Language is one of the most important characteristics that differentiate human beings from animals. It is the carrier of human thinking and accumulated and passed-down knowledge.

请注意，该句结尾处的“知识凝练和传承的载体”实际上是“凝练和传承知识的载体”，所以译文将语序进行了调整，这样更符合逻辑。

参考译文

Natural language processing (NLP) is a branch of artificial intelligence (AI), aimed for intelligent processing of natural languages with the computer. Basic NLP is done to different hierarchical levels of languages, including phonology, morphology, lexicology, syntax, semantics, pragmatics, and discourse. It has been applied to multiple natural language processing tasks downstream, including machine translation, dialog, Q&A, and document summarization.

By studying NLP, scientists aim to enable the machine to understand human language, so that it can communicate with human in a natural language and thus have its “intelligence.” In the era of AI, the computer is expected to have the ability to see, hear, speak, and act. Language is one of the most important characteristics that differentiate human beings from animals. It is the carrier of human thinking and accumulated and passed-down knowledge. In AI, NLP is aimed to make the machine understand and generate human language and thus communicate with human beings fluently.

第四模块：翻译练习

1. 英译中

Classical computing using digital symbols is reaching its limits. It is undeniable that computing’s historic exponential performance increases have improved the human condition. Yet such increases are a thing of the past due in large part to the constraints of physics and how today’s systems are constructed. Hardware device designers struggle to eliminate the effects of nanometer-scale thermodynamic fluctuations, and the soaring cost of fabrication plants has eliminated all but a few companies as a source of future chips. Software developers’ abilities to imagine and program effective computational abstractions and implementations are clearly challenged in complex domains like economic systems, ecological systems, medicine, social systems, warfare, and autonomous vehicles. Machine learning techniques, such as deep neural networks, can help but their capabilities are limited.

2. 中译英

噪音对人体最直接的危害体现在听力损伤，例如长期处于反复性的噪音暴露环境，或者一次性在超分贝噪音环境中暴露过长时间，就会造成感应神经性耳聋。噪声除了对耳朵和听力的直接损伤外，还会对我们的眼睛和视力造成影响。相关实验表明，当噪声达到90分贝时，人的视觉细胞的敏感性就会下降，识别弱光反应时间延长；噪声达到95分贝时，有40%的人瞳孔放大，视线模糊；而噪声达到115分贝时，大多数人的眼球对光亮度的适应都有不同程度的减弱。所以，长时间处于噪声环境中的人很容易发生眼疲劳、眼痛、眼花和视物流泪等现象。

第七单元　法律

第一模块：法律翻译概述

法律文体主要包括法律条文和合同。其中法律条文是现代国家的规范性法律文件，可分为规范性条文和非规范性条文。规范性条文是直接表述法律规范的条文，如法律规则和法律原则；非规范性条文是指不直接规定法律规范的条文，而规定某些法律技术内容，如专门术语的界定、公布机关和时间、生效日期等，非规范性条文不可能独立存在，而是附属于规范性法律条文。合同是指两个或两个以上当事人达成的协议，旨在明确各方的权利和义务关系，是具有法律约束力的承诺或契约。法律文体是一种严肃正式的文体，无论中英文，其语言表达准确、正式、客观，用词专业、规范，句式结构比较复杂，措辞严谨，行文严密。

一、英文法律文本的文体特点及其翻译

（一）用词特点

英语法律文本常用一些法律专业术语，具有明确的特定法律含义，有的表达复杂的法律概念。这些法律术语有的是地道的英语，但也有一些外来词，如拉丁语和法语等，如appeal（上诉）、defendant（被告）、plaintiff（原告）、demurrer（抗辩）、*affidavit*（拉丁语，证词）、*inter alia*（拉丁语，除了别的事情之外）、*ex parte*（拉丁语，单方面的）、*voir dire*（法语，预先审查）等等。这些术语需要译者找到对应的中文表达，所以在翻译法律文本时，要勤于查词典。特别是一些普通词汇出现在法律文本中，查阅词典时要查阅其法律释义，找到对应的中文法律用词。

英语法律文体常用正式词汇，从而保证法律文书严肃、正式的风格，汉语译文也要体现这种风格，因此也需要使用表达正式的译文。下表是一些口语词汇或普通词汇与法律常用正式词汇对照表（附汉语正式表达）：

日常用词	法律文本用词	中文
about	pertain to/in respect to	关于……
above	said/aforesaid	上述的
according to	under/as per/in accordance with/subject to	按照，根据
add	supplement	增加，添加
allow	approve, permit	允许，批准
ask	require, request	请求，申请
before	prior to	在……之前
begin	commence	开始
buy	purchase, procure	购买
change	variation/alteration/modification	变更
duty	obligation, liability	责任，义务
end	terminate	终止
explain	construe	解释
from	as from	自……日起
give	assign/transfer	转让
given the fact that	whereas	鉴于
have a meeting	convene	召集会议
instead of	in lieu of	代替
power	authority	权力
temporary	interim	临时的

英语法律文本中经常使用here、there和where为词根加介词构成的复合词汇，如hereby、therefrom和whereof等，这些词属于古体词，多用作副词，在句子中做状语或定语，表示时间、地点、方式或条件等。请看下面的例子：

例1

No will or any part *thereof*, which is in any manner revoked, shall be revived otherwise than by the re-execution *thereof* or by a codicil executed in accordance with section 5 and showing an intention to revive it.

遗嘱的全部或任何部分内容，以任何方式撤销后，除非按照第5条重新签立或加入按照第5条签立的遗嘱更改附件，并表明恢复遗嘱效力的意愿，否则该遗嘱的全部或任何部分内容均不可恢复效力。

该例原文有两处使用了thereof，相当于of+the will，翻译时根据上下文进行了处理。

例2

The Seller shall supply to the Buyer complete designs and technical documentation (*hereinafter* referred to as "Technical Documentation").

卖方应向买方提供完整的设计与技术资料（以下简称"技术资料"）。

hereinafter相当于in this contract+after this section，一般翻译为"以下"。

例3

The terms shall include a provision *whereby*, in the event of any claim in respect of which the Contractor would be entitled to receive indemnity under the policy being brought or made against the Employer, the insurer will indemnify the Employer against such claims and any costs, charges, and expenses *in respect thereof*.

保险条款中应包括这样一条规定，即：如果承包人凭借不利于雇主的保险单有资格向雇主提出有关索赔，则保险人应保障雇主不承担与此有关的任何索赔、诉讼费、指控和有关开支。

例3中的whereby就是by the provision，而in respect thereof 即in respect of the matter referred to in the clause。翻译时，没有将whereby译为"根据此规定"，而直接使用了"即"，这是因为前面刚刚说到"规定"，in respect thereof 根据上下文译为"与此有关的"。

法律文体中shall是使用最为频繁的情态动词，表示义务、职责、权利和许诺等，相当于should、must、have to、be required to，所以翻译时要根据上下文译成"应""须"等，有时也可省略不译。请看下面的例子：

例4

Payment *shall* be effected within seven days after receipt of the shipping documents stipulated under Clause 10 of this Contract.

买方须在收到本合同第10条规定的装船单据后7天内付款。

例5

The Convention *shall not* affect the application of any international convention or national law relating to the regulation and control of transport operations.

本公约不得影响有关运输业务管理的任何国际公约或国内法的实施。

例6

Party A *shall* pay the interest on its long-term letter of credit, and pay the interest on the loans due to be rendered by Party B in advance. The annual interest rate is agreed upon at 5%.

甲方所开的远期信用证及乙方所预付的贷款利息应由甲方承担，双方议定的年利率为百分之五。

例7

The Board *shall* have jurisdiction and powers as are conferred on it by this or any other Ordinance.

仲裁处拥有本条例或任何其他条例授予的司法管辖权及其他权力。

以上四个例子中，例4中的shall译成了"须"，用以强调买方的义务；例5中的shall not译成了"不得"，有"必须不能"之意；例6中的shall译成了"应"；例7中的shall省译。

英语法律文体中常见到两个近义词并列使用，这种用法显示了法律语言的严肃性以及严密性，如果两个词意思基本一样，翻译时则译成一个汉语词，如sole and exclusive（单一）、null and void（无效）；如果两个词意思相似但稍有差别，则译成两个汉语词，如obligation and liability（义务与责任）、sell or transfer（出售或转让）。

（二）句式特点

英语法律文体的句式特点首先是长句。有些译者认为法律文体难翻译，就在于句子太长。法律文体句子之所以比较长，就是因为其表达严密、完整，同时要明确权利和义务，从句和插入语使用较多。翻译长句和前面单元讲过的一样，先要对句子进行分析，厘清其中的逻辑关系。请看下面的例子：

七

例8

Everyone, as a member of society, has the right to social security and is entitled to realization, through national effort and international co-operation and in accordance with the organization and resources of each State, of the economic, social, and cultural rights indispensable for his dignity and the free development of his personality.

每个人作为社会的一员，有权享有社会保障，有权通过国家努力和国际合作并依照各国的组织和资源条件，实现其个人尊严和人格自由发展所必需的经济、社会和文化方面的各种权利。

例9

A person who disposes of or otherwise deals with any property specified in a notice under subsection (1) or a bank or deposit-taking company which pays any money to a person specified in a copy of a notice under subsection (1A) other than in accordance with the consent of the Commissioner shall be guilty of an offence and shall be liable on conviction to a fine of HK$50,000 or the value of the property disposed of or otherwise dealt with, whichever is greater, and to imprisonment for three years.

未经专员同意，任何人如对按第（1）款规定所发通知中说明的财产进行处置或以其他方式处理，或任何银行或接受存款的公司将款项支付给根据第（1A）款规定送达的通知书副本指定的人员，即构成犯罪，一经定罪，将处罚款50,000港币，或处以与所处置或以其他方式处理的财产价值相等的罚款，以两款项中大额为准，并判处监禁三年。

例10

During the Term and for ten years thereafter, Buyer shall keep confidential and not disclose to others or use for any purpose, other than as authorized by this Agreement, all "Confidential Information" that was provided to Buyer or its Affiliates or its employees or representatives.

在协议期限内以及其后十年内，买方应对提供给买方或其下属机构或其雇员或其代表的所有"保密信息"严格保密，不得出于任何目的向他人披露或使用这些信息，本协议授权的情况除外。

例11

In the event that any Party fails to make any contribution to the registered capital of the Joint Venture company as required by Article 7, interest shall accrue and be payable to the Joint Venture company by such Party on the value

of each late contribution from its scheduled payment date until the date when such contribution is actually made, at a rate equal to 2 percentage points over the highest annual rate of interest announced by the Bank of China for loans in Renminbi or US Dollars for the same period.
若一方不按照第7条规定缴纳合营企业的注册资本，该方应就每次迟缴金额向合营企业支付自应出资之日起至实际出资之日止的利息，其利率按同期中国银行公布的人民币或美元贷款的最高利率加2个百分点计算。

英语法律文体的句式经常会使用一些表示条件的从句，如if和in case引导的条件状语从句，或者用in the event后面加that引导的同位语从句，抑或是使用where引导的条件状语从句。这些从句因为都表示条件，所以可以译为“如……”或“若……”。请看下面的例子：

例12

If damages of the goods are found, or the specifications and/or quantity are not in conformity with the stipulations in this Contract, except when the responsibilities lie with Insurance Company or Shipping Company, the Buyer shall, within 30 days after arrival of the goods at the port of destination, claim against the Seller, or reject the goods according to the inspection certificate issued by China Commodity Inspection Bureau.
如发现货物残损或规格和/或数量与合同规定不符，除保险公司或船运公司的责任外，买方须在货物到达目的港后30日内凭中国商品检验局出具的检验证书向卖方索赔或拒收该货。

例13

Where the sum payable is expressed in words and also in figures, and there is a discrepancy between the two, the sum denoted by the words is the amount payable.
若应付金额同时用文字和数字表示但两者存在差异，应以文字表示的金额为准。

例14

In the event that the taxpayer prevents a withholding agent from fulfilling its obligations, the withholding agent shall promptly report the case in question to the tax authorities.
若纳税人拒绝扣缴义务人履行代扣义务，扣缴义务人应立即报告税务机关处理。

以上三个例子中分别有if引导的条件状语从句、where引导的条件状语从句和in the event后面加that引导的同位语从句，实际上都暗含假设的意思，所以均将带有从句的部分译成了汉语的“如/若……”。

被动句也是英语法律文体中常用的句式之一，因为法律文本中有时不必说出动作的发出者，有时为了强调动作的承受者，两种情况下均使用动作的承受者做主语，于是就使用被动语态。法律文体中的被动语态大多也需要译成汉语的主动语态，少数情况下可以译为被动。请看下面的例子：

例15

The prices stated are based on current freight rates, and any increase or decrease in freight rates at the time of shipment shall be the responsibility of the Buyer, with the Seller assuming the payment of all transportation charges to the point or place of delivery.

合同价格是以现行运费计算，装运时运费的增减均属买方，卖方则承担至交货地的全部运费。

例16

No money shall be drawn from the treasury but in consequence of appropriations made by law; and a regular statement and account of the receipts and expenditures of all public money shall be published from time to time.

除法律规定外，不得从国库中提取任何款项；一切公款收支的报告和账目应经常公布。

例17

If the Agreement is held null and void, both parties shall terminate the Agreement.

如果该协议视为无效，合作双方将终止协议。

以上三个例子的被动语态均转译为汉语的主动语态，例15和例17没有改变原文主要语序，例16则译成汉语的无主句。下面的例子中被动语态用by引出动作的发出者，可以直接译为被动语态“由……”。

例18

During the intervals between meetings of the Board of Directors, the affairs of the Corporation shall be administered by an Executive Committee consisting of the President, five Directors selected by the Board of Directors, and, without vote, the First Vice President and Chief Executive Officer.

董事会会议间隔期间，公司事务由执行委员会管理，执行委员会由总裁、董事会选出的五名董事及第一副总裁兼首席执行官组成。第一副总裁兼首席执行官无需经董事会表决即成为执行委员会成员。

二、中文法律文本的文体特点及其翻译

（一）用词特点

中文法律文本常使用一些法律专业术语与相关领域的术语，这些术语翻译时需要找到英文的对应表达。请看下面的例子：

例19

本协议于双方签字后且乙方在签字后五个工作日内向甲方缴纳履约保证金后生效，如乙方在本协议履行过程中出现违约责任，甲方可直接从履约保证金中予以扣划。

This Agreement shall come into effect on condition that both parties have signed this Agreement and Party B pays Party A the *performance bond* within five working days after signing of this Agreement. In case Party B is liable for *breach of contract* during the performance of this Agreement, Party A is entitled to deduct the performance bond as compensation.

例20

农村集体经济组织实行家庭承包经营为基础、统分结合的双层经营体制。农村中的生产、供销、信用、消费等各种形式的合作经济，是社会主义劳动群众集体所有制经济。参加农村集体经济组织的劳动者，有权在法律规定的范围内经营自留地、自留山、家庭副业和饲养自留畜。

Rural *collective economic* organizations shall practice a two-tiered system of both unified and separate operations with *household contract management* as its basis. Rural economic cooperatives—producer, supply and marketing, credit and consumer cooperatives—are part of the socialist *economy under collective ownership* by the working people. Working people who belong to rural collective economic organizations shall have the right, within the scope prescribed by law, to farm cropland and hillsides allotted to them for their private use, engage in *household sideline production*, and raise privately owned livestock.

以上两个例子中既有法律文本本身的术语，如“违约责任”，又有相关领域的术语，如“履约保证金”“集体经济”“家庭承包经营”“集体所有制经济”和“家庭副业”等。特别是后面几个词均具有中国特色，所以要注意其英文表达。

汉语法律文本还经常使用一些文言词汇，显得正式、庄重，如“本”“若/如”等。这些词汇在英语中没有对应的古体词，但可以通过行文中其他古体词来表现原文正式、庄重的语气。

例21

未经甲方的书面同意，乙方不得将本协议（包括附件）各项权利及义务全部或者部分转让给第三方。

Without the written consent of Party A, the rights and obligations including attachments stipulated herein *shall not be* completely or partially transferred by Party B to the third party.

该例中，“未经”“不得”等字眼偏文雅，翻译时只能翻译意思，但是译文中其他一些词非常正式，如consent、herein，这样就能够保证原文庄重和正式的语气得以再现。

例22

根据本法第五十五条规定管辖案件时，本法第五十六条规定的执法、司法机关依法行使相关权力，其为决定采取强制措施、侦查措施和司法裁判而签发的法律文书在香港特别行政区具有法律效力。对于驻香港特别行政区维护国家安全公署依法采取的措施，有关机构、组织和个人必须遵从。

When exercising jurisdiction over cases pursuant to Article 55 of this Law, the law enforcement and judicial authorities referred to in Article 56 of this Law shall exercise powers in accordance with the law. The legal documents issued by these authorities on their decisions to take mandatory and investigation measures and on their judicial decisions shall have legal force in the Hong Kong Special Administrative Region. The institutions, organisations and individuals concerned must comply with measures taken by the Office for Safeguarding National Security of the Central People's Government in the Hong Kong Special Administrative Region in accordance with the law.

该句中“本”和“其”属于文言词汇，虽然这样的词汇在英文中没有对应的古体词，但是可以通过其他词来再现原文的语气，该例译文就使用了pursuant to和in accordance with这样的正式表达再现了原文的语气。

（二）句式特点

中文法律文体中也经常使用长句，但由于中文长句会带有很多并列小分句，所以读起来并不复杂，但翻译时需要厘清并列小分句之间真正的逻辑关系，找到主要结构和次要结构，再进行翻译。请看下面的例子：

例23

为坚定不移并全面准确贯彻“一国两制”、“港人治港”、高度自治的方针，维护国家安全，防范、制止和惩治与香港特别行政区有关的分裂国家、颠覆国家政权、组织实施恐怖活动和勾结外国或者境外势力危害国家安全等犯罪，保持香港特别行政区的繁荣和稳定，保障香港特别行政区居民的合法权益，根据中华人民共和国宪法、中华人民共和国香港特别行政区基本法和全国人民代表大会关于建立健全香港特别行政区维护国家安全的法律制度和执行机制的决定，制定本法。

This Law is enacted, in accordance with the Constitution of the People's Republic of China, the Basic Law of the Hong Kong Special Administrative Region of the People's Republic of China, and the Decision of the National People's Congress on Establishing and Improving the Legal System and Enforcement Mechanisms for Safeguarding National Security in the Hong Kong Special Administrative Region, for the purpose of ensuring the resolute, full and faithful implementation of the policy of One Country, Two Systems under which the people of Hong Kong administer Hong Kong with a high degree of autonomy; safeguarding national security; preventing, suppressing and imposing punishment for the offences of secession, subversion, organisation and perpetration of terrorist activities, and collusion with a foreign country or with external elements to endanger national security in relation to the Hong Kong Special Administrative Region; maintaining prosperity and stability of the Hong Kong Special Administrative Region; and protecting the lawful rights and interests of the residents of the Hong Kong Special Administrative Region.

仔细阅读原文，会发现这句话虽然长，但主结构很简单，就是“制定本法”，所以这一部分就是英语译文的主结构。从开头到“保障香港特别行政区居民的合法权益”是目的，“根据中华人民共和国宪法、中华人民共和国香港特别行政区基本法和全国人民代表大会关于建立健全香港特别行政区维护国家安全的法律制度和执行机制的决定”是“制定本法”的依据，这两部分都是状语，但要注意将短一点的状语放在长一点的状语前面。

例24

甲方积极支持乙方的市场推广活动，乙方需要甲方配合与支持时，甲方应全力支持并指导，涉及经费需双方书面确定各自承担的比例。

Party A shall take the initiative to support Party B in marketing activities. When Party B needs Party A's cooperation and support, Party A shall provide Party B with full supports and guidance, with the proportion of expenses to be borne by each party determined by both parties.

仔细阅读例24，会发现“甲方积极支持乙方的市场推广活动”与后面的关系并不十分密切，所以翻译时可以考虑拆句。后半部分则可以译成一句话，也比较长，符合英文合同的句式结构特点。

中文法律文体为显示客观、公正、正式，常用无主句。为准确传达原文的语气，翻译时可以译成英语被动句。请看下面的例子：

例25

为了加强城市居民委员会的建设，由城市居民群众依法办理群众自己的事情，促进城市基层社会主义民主和城市社会主义物质文明、精神文明建设的发展，根据宪法，制定本法。

Pursuant to the Constitution, this Law is formulated with a view to improving the urban residents committee as an institution, enabling urban residents to administer their own affairs in accordance with the law, promoting socialist democracy at the grassroots level in cities, and furthering socialist material development and the building of an advanced socialist culture and ideology in urban areas.

例26

在正常情况下，乙方拒不交货，则每天处以货款总额20%的罚金；质量不合格，则重新酬价；如逾期交货，则每天处以5%的滞纳金。

Normally, Party B, if it refuses to deliver the said goods, shall be subject to a penalty per day equaling twenty percent (20%) of the total value of the goods; if the goods fail to have the expected quality, the price shall be redefined; if the delivery is delayed, a penalty for the delay shall be charged at a rate equal to five percent (5%) per day.

例25中主结构是“制定本法”，属于无主句，因此译成被动语态。例26的第一个分号后面两个并列结构也都是无主句，为体现客观公正的语气，可译成被动语态。

中文法律文体还经常使用“的”字结构，通常用来表示假设，一般情况下，这些结构可以译成if/in case/where引导的条件状语从句。但如果“的”字结构代表的是名词短语，就需要译成定语从句，有时译为whoever引导的主语从句。请看下面的例子：

例27

货物运输需要办理审批、检验等手续的，托运人应当将办理完有关手续的文件提交承运人。

Where a freight transport is subject to approval or inspection, the consignor shall submit to the carrier the documents showing the completion of the relevant formalities.

例28

有下列情形之一的，不得就损失索赔。

Where one of the following happens, no claim shall be requested.

例29

国有公司、企业的工作人员，由于严重不负责任或者滥用职权，造成国有公司、企业破产或者严重损失，致使国家利益遭受重大损失的，处三年以下有期徒刑或者拘役。

Where an employee of a state-owned company or enterprise is seriously irresponsible or abuses the office, causing its bankruptcy or serious losses to the state-owned company or enterprise, and causing heavy losses to the interests of the state, he shall be sentenced to fixed-term imprisonment of not more than three years or limited incarceration.

例30

组织、策划、实施分裂国家、破坏国家统一的，对首要分子或者罪行重大的，处无期徒刑或者十年以上有期徒刑。

Whoever organizes, plots, or acts to split the country or undermine national reunification, the ringleader, or the one whose crime is grave, shall be sentenced to life imprisonment or fixed-term imprisonment of not less than ten years.

以上四个例子充分说明汉语法律文体中“的”字结构使用频繁，翻译时根据“的”字结构的意思以及与行文其他部分之间的关系选择使用英语where、that/who 和whoever引导的从句。

三、法律文本翻译原则与策略归纳

综上，无论是英语法律文本还是中文法律文本，都显示出其严谨、正式、客观的语气，这些体现在词汇和句式结构上。因此，翻译法律文本时要遵循以下原则：(1) 用词规范，准确传达专业意思；(2) 措辞严谨、正式，再现原文的语气；(3) 译文完整，注重细节；(4) 句法正确，语气贴切；(5) 表达清晰，逻辑正确，行文通顺；(6) 语态使用合理。法律文本的翻译策略可总结归纳如下：

英译中

	英文法律文本的文体特点	翻译策略
词汇	法律专业术语	在汉语中找到对应术语。
	正式、严肃词汇	汉语译文也要正式、严肃，多用文言词汇。
	古体词	理解古体词代表的意思，根据上下文处理。
	情态动词shall	译成汉语的“应”“须”，有时省译。
	近义词连用	意思相同时译成一个汉语词，意思相近但有差别时，译成两个词。
句式	长句	先分析逻辑关系，再着手翻译，确保行文逻辑清晰，语言流畅。
	条件句、in the event后面加同位语从句、where引导的状语从句	译成中文的“如……”或“若……”。
	被动句	大部分转译为汉语的主动语态，个别情况下保留被动语态。

中译英

	中文法律文本的文体特点	翻译策略
词汇	法律和相关领域专业术语	在英语中找到对应表达。
	文言词汇	通过使用英语的正式词汇和古体词体现原文的语气。

（待续）

（续表）

	中文法律文本的文体特点	翻译策略
句式	长句	先分析出主从结构，再进行翻译。有些长句前后关系不密切时，可拆句。
	无主句	一般译为英语的被动句。
	“的”字结构	根据意思和逻辑关系翻译成英语中表示条件的状语从句，有时译为定语从句或其他名词性从句。

第二模块：英文法律语篇汉译解析

原文

Termination of the agreement

1. Subject to the earlier termination under clause 3 below, this agreement shall continue for five years from the date of signature unless and until terminated by either party giving to the other not less than six months' written notice expiring on or after or any time after the first anniversary date of the signing of this agreement.

2. Without prejudice to the general nature of clause 1, either party may terminate this agreement with effect from the end of the first year by not less than one month's notice in writing to the other.

3. Either party shall be entitled to terminate this agreement forthwith by giving notice to the other:

3.1 If either party remains in breach of its obligations under this agreement 30 days after receipt of a notice in writing from the other sent by registered post or facsimile specifying the breach and requiring the same to be remedied;

3.2 Immediately if either party shall become insolvent or unable to pay its debts within the meaning of section 123 of the Insolvency Act 1986 or shall make an arrangement with its creditors or being an individual becomes bankrupt or unable to pay its debts within the meaning of section 268 of the Insolvency Act 1986 or enters into a voluntary arrangement with its creditors or it carries out or undergoes any analogous act or proceedings under foreign law.

4. The Company shall be entitled to terminate this agreement forthwith in the event that the Distributor shall:

4.1 fail to meet the purchase requirements set out herein;

4.2 fail to pay the Company for each consignment of Products within 45 days of consignment;

4.3 be, in the reasonable opinion of the Company, likely to become insolvent or unable to pay its debts or commit some other act of insolvency.

七

翻译解析

本篇是合同的节选，属于典型的英语法律文体。下面详细分析本篇的翻译。

1. 英语合同常用语

英语合同中经常使用subject to和without prejudice to这样的表达，subject to一般翻译为“在遵守……规定的前提下”“在符合……的情况下”或“受制于……的规定”，根据具体情况选择；without prejudice to强调不要影响或损害有关规定的事物，可以译为“在不损害……的原则下”或“在不影响……的前提下”。本篇的例子如下：

（1）subject to the earlier termination under clause 3 below：除根据本协议第三条提前终止协议外

（2）without prejudice to the general nature of clause 1：在不违反第一条基本性质的前提下

2. under的翻译

英语法律文体常使用under表示法律条文、合同或协议条款的规定，不少译文将其翻译为“……下的”，实际上这一翻译并不符合汉语的表达习惯。建议翻译为“……规定的”或“根据……”，具体视上下文而定。例如本篇出现的两个例子：

（1）obligations under this agreement：本协议中规定的义务

（2）any analogous act or proceedings under foreign law：根据外国法律采取类似的行动或卷入类似诉讼

3. 英语名词短语转译为汉语动词短语

如前文讲到，英语法律文体中常用一些名词短语，往往是由动词加后缀变来的名词加上其逻辑宾语或主语构成，实际上这个名词的动作性比较强，译成汉语时建议转译为动词短语，使其更符合汉语的表达习惯。

（1）the signing of this agreement

这里的名词signing实际上与后面的agreement构成逻辑上的动宾关系，所以应该译为“签订本协议”。

（2）breach of its obligations under this agreement

这里的breach是名词，与后面的obligations构成逻辑上的动宾关系，所以建议翻译成“违反本协议中规定的义务”。

（3）receipt of a notice

这里的receipt是名词，但与后面的notice构成逻辑上的动宾关系，所以建议译为“收到通知”。

4. 长句

本篇中有几个长句，符合法律文体的句式结构特点。翻译时需要根据前文讲过的方法，先对句子进行分析，厘清其中的逻辑关系，然后再进行翻译。

（1）Subject to the earlier termination under clause 3 below, this agreement shall continue for five years from the date of signature unless and until terminated by either party giving to the other not less than six months' written notice expiring on or after or any time after the first anniversary date of the signing of this agreement.

这句话的主结构是this agreement shall continue for five years from the date of signature，之后从unless开始到句尾说明了具体条件。分析完结构后，再进行翻译。拟译如下：

除根据本协议第三条提前终止协议外，本协议的有效期为协议签订之日后的五年，除非一方在签订本协议一周年之际或之后的某一时间提前六个月发出书面通知终止本协议。

（2）Without prejudice to the general nature of clause 1, either party may terminate this agreement with effect from the end of the first year by not less than one month's notice in writing to the other.

这句话相对于上面一句并不十分复杂，主结构是either party may terminate this agreement，翻译时只需要调整一下状语with effect from the end of the first year by not less than one month's notice in writing to the other的位置。整句话拟译如下：

在不违反第一条基本性质的前提下，任何一方均可通过提前一个月向另一方发出书面通知而在协议生效第一年后终止本协议。

（3）If either party remains in breach of its obligations under this agreement 30 days after receipt of a notice in writing from the other sent by registered post or facsimile specifying the breach and requiring the same to be remedied.

这部分实际上只是一个条件状语从句，但里面的内容比较丰富，说明通知的形式、寄送方式以及内容，所以要细细梳理。拟译如下：

（如果）某一方违反本协议中规定的义务，在收到另一方以挂号邮寄或传真发出的列明违反事项并要求对此进行赔偿的通知30日后，依然违反其在本协议中应承担的义务。

（4）Immediately if either party shall become insolvent or unable to pay its debts within the meaning of section 123 of the Insolvency Act 1986 or shall make an arrangement with its creditors or being an individual becomes bankrupt or unable to pay its debts within the meaning of section 268 of the Insolvency Act 1986 or enters into a voluntary arrangement with its creditors or it carries out or undergoes any analogous act or proceedings under foreign law.

这一部分也是条件状语，里面假设一方遇到的问题，包括破产、无力偿还债务或其他情况。拟译如下：

（如果）一方根据1986年《破产法》第123条的规定应破产或无力偿还债务，或应与其债权人形成协议，或者作为个人，根据1986年《破产法》第268条的规定破产或无力偿还其债务，或自愿与其债权人达成协议或者根据外国法律采取类似的行动或卷入类似诉讼。

5. 语气

翻译时请注意整篇合同的语气，汉语译文的措辞要注意庄重、严肃、正式。

参考译文

终止协议

1. 除根据本协议第三条提前终止协议外，本协议的有效期为协议签订之日后的五年，除非一方在签订本协议一周年之际或之后的某一时间提前六个月发出书面通知终止本协议。

2. 在不违反第一条基本性质的前提下，任何一方均可通过提前一个月向另一方发出书面通知而在协议生效第一年后终止本协议。

3. 如果出现以下任一情况，任何一方均有权通过向另一方发出书面通知而立即终止本协议：

3.1 某一方违反本协议中规定的义务，在收到另一方以挂号邮寄或传真发出的列明违反事项并要求对此进行赔偿的通知30日后，依然违反其在本协议中应承担的义务；

3.2 一方根据1986年《破产法》第123条的规定应破产或无力偿还债务，或应与其债权人形成协议，或者作为个人，根据1986年《破产法》第268条的规定破产或无力偿还其债务，或自愿与其债权人达成协议或者根据外国法律采取类似的行动或卷入类似诉讼。

4. 如果经销商发生如下情况，公司有权立即终止本协议：

4.1 未能满足本协议规定的购买要求；

4.2 在发货后45日内未能向公司支付货款；

4.3 根据公司的合理判断，可能会破产或无力偿还其债务或违反了其他有关破产的法律。

第三模块：中文法律语篇英译解析

原文

第十九条　在公司中，根据中国共产党章程的规定，设立中国共产党的组织，开展党的活动。公司应当为党组织的活动提供必要条件。

第二十条　公司股东应当遵守法律、行政法规和公司章程，依法行使股东权利，不得滥用股东权利损害公司或者其他股东的利益；不得滥用公司法人独立地位和股东有限责任损害公司债权人的利益。公司股东滥用股东权利给公司或者其他股东造成损失的，应当依法承担赔偿责任。公司股东滥用公司法人独立地位和股东有限责任，逃避债务，严重损害公司债权人利益的，应当对公司债务承担连带责任。

第二十一条　公司的控股股东、实际控制人、董事、监事、高级管理人员不得利用其关联关系损害公司利益。违反前款规定，给公司造成损失的，应当承担赔偿责任。

第二十二条　公司股东会或者股东大会、董事会的决议内容违反法律、行政法规的无效。股东会或者股东大会、董事会的会议召集程序、表决方式违反法律、行政法规或者公司章程，或者决议内容违反公司章程的，股东可以自决议作出之日起六十日内，请求人民法院撤销。股东依照前款规定提起诉讼的，人民法院可以应公司的请求，要求股东提供相应担保。公司根据股东会或者股东大会、董事会决议已办理变更登记的，人民法院宣告该决议无效或者撤销该决议后，公司应当向公司登记机关申请撤销变更登记。

翻译解析

本篇选自《中华人民共和国公司法》，属于比较典型的法律文体。本篇翻译时主要有以下几点特别值得注意。

1. 专业术语和专有名词

本篇有一些关于公司结构和法律方面的专业表达，还有几个专有名词，翻译时需要找到最准确的表达方式。列举如下：

（1）中国共产党章程：Constitution of the Communist Party of China
（2）股东：shareholder
（3）章程：bylaw
（4）法人：legal person
（5）债权人：creditor
（6）连带责任：joint liabilities
（7）控股股东：controlling shareholder
（8）实际控制人：actual controller
（9）董事：director
（10）监事：supervisor
（11）高级管理人员：senior management
（12）股东会：shareholders' meeting
（13）股东大会：shareholders' assembly
（14）董事会：board of directors
（15）人民法院：the people's court
（16）变更登记：modification registration
（17）登记机关：registration authority

2. 英语同义词或近义词

本篇有的地方翻译时可使用英语法律文体中连用的同义词或近义词。例如：

公司股东会或者股东大会、董事会的决议内容违反法律、行政法规的无效。

这里的“无效”可以译成前文提到过的null and void。整句话拟译为：

A resolution of the shareholders' meeting, shareholders' assembly or board of directors of the company that is in violation of any law or administrative regulation shall be *null and void*.

3. “的”字结构

本篇有多处使用了“的”字结构，这些“的”字结构可根据其意思进行灵活处理，有的可以处理成条件状语从句，有的可以处理成定语从句。

（1）违反前款规定，给公司造成损失的，应当承担赔偿责任。

这里的“的”字结构较短，结合上下文会发现其意思是“违反前款规定，给公司造成损失的人/股东/董事……”，所以可以考虑使用定语从句。拟译如下：

Anyone who causes any loss to the company due to violating the preceding paragraph shall be liable for the compensation.

（2）股东依照前款规定提起诉讼的，人民法院可以应公司的请求，要求股东提供相应担保。

这句话中的“的”字结构明显是条件，因此可以考虑使用if或where引导的条件状语从句。拟译如下：

If/Where the shareholders initiate a lawsuit under the preceding paragraph, the people's court shall, at the request of the company, demand that the shareholders provide corresponding guaranty.

（3）公司根据股东会或者股东大会、董事会决议已办理变更登记的，人民法院宣告该决议无效或者撤销该决议后，公司应当向公司登记机关申请撤销变更登记。

这句话中除了“的”字结构表示条件，仔细分析后会发现，“人民法院宣告该决议无效或者撤销该决议后”实际上也是条件，所以建议将“的”字结构译为where从句，后面译为if从句。整句话拟译如下：

Where a company has, according to the resolution of the shareholders' meeting, shareholders' assembly or board of directors, completed the modification registration, if the people's court declares the resolution null and void or revokes the resolution, the company shall file an application with the company registration authority for revoking the modification registration.

4. 长句

本篇的长句不是很多，前面讲的含“的”字结构的句子有的也比较长，但既然讲过，这里不再重复。除此之外，还有下面两句比较长：

（1）公司股东应当遵守法律、行政法规和公司章程，依法行使股东权利，不得滥用股东权利损害公司或者其他股东的利益；不得滥用公司法人独立地位和股东有限责任损害公司债权人的利益。

这句话比较长，可以根据句意进行拆分。通过“应当……”“不得……”“不得……”三个关键词可以发现，这句话包含肯定和否定的两层含义，不宜放在一个英文句子中，建议拆分成两句，语义会更清晰。拟译如下：

The shareholders of a company shall abide by the laws, administrative regulations and bylaw and shall exercise the shareholder's rights under the law. None of them may harm the interests of the company or of other shareholders by abusing the shareholder's rights, or harm the interests of any creditor of the company by abusing the independent status of legal person or the shareholder's limited liabilities.

（2）股东会或者股东大会、董事会的会议召集程序、表决方式违反法律、行政法规或者公司章程，或者决议内容违反公司章程的，股东可以自决议作出之日起六十日内，请求人民法院撤销。

这句话包含一个“的”字结构表条件，“或者决议内容违反公司章程的”之前的内容实际上也是一个条件，所以考虑使用并列条件状语从句。整句话拟译如下：

If the procedure for calling a shareholders' meeting or shareholders' assembly or board of directors, or the voting form, is in violation of any law, administrative regulation or the bylaw, or if a resolution is in violation of the bylaw of the company, the shareholders may, within 60 days from the day when the resolution is made, request the people's court to revoke it.

5. 情态动词shall和不定代词any

翻译本篇时，需要注意很多地方要使用情态动词shall，来明确法律规定的义务。特别是原文多处“应当”均需翻译成shall。另外，英语法律文本中常用any来说明任何人、任何情况等，符合法律文体的语气，翻译时也要注意使用。具体请参见参考译文，此不赘述。

参考译文

Article 19 The Communist Party of China may, according to the Constitution of the Communist Party of China, establish its branches in companies to carry out activities of the Party. The company shall provide necessary conditions to facilitate the activities of the Party.

Article 20 The shareholders of a company shall abide by the laws, administrative regulations and bylaw and shall exercise the shareholder's rights under the law. None of them may harm the interests of the company or of other shareholders by abusing the shareholder's rights, or harm the interests of any creditor of the company by abusing the independent status of legal person or the shareholder's limited liabilities. Where any of the shareholders of a company causes any loss to the company or to other shareholders by abusing the shareholder's rights, it shall be liable for compensation. Where any of the shareholders of a company evades the payment of its debts by abusing the independent status of legal person or the shareholder's limited liabilities, if it seriously harms the interests of any creditor, it shall bear several and joint liabilities for the debts of the company.

Article 21 Neither the controlling shareholder, nor the actual controller, nor any of the directors, supervisors or senior management of the company may harm the interests of the company by taking advantage of its connection relationship. Anyone who causes any loss to the company due to violating the preceding paragraph shall be liable for the compensation.

Article 22 A resolution of the shareholders' meeting, shareholders' assembly or board of directors of the company that is in violation of any law or administrative regulation shall be null and void. If the procedure for calling a shareholders' meeting or shareholders' assembly or board of directors, or the voting form, is in violation of any law, administrative regulation or the bylaw, or if a resolution is in violation of the bylaw of the company, the shareholders may, within 60 days from the day when the resolution is made, request the people's court to revoke it. If the shareholders initiate a lawsuit under the preceding paragraph, the people's court shall, at the request of the company, demand that the shareholders provide corresponding guaranty. Where a company has, according to the resolution of the shareholders' meeting, shareholders' assembly or board of directors, completed the modification registration, if the people's court declares the resolution null and void or revokes the resolution, the company shall file an application with the company registration authority for revoking the modification registration.

第四模块：翻译练习

1. 英译中

If Control of the Distributor is acquired at any time by any person or group of connected persons not having Control of the Distributor at the date of this agreement, the Distributor shall forthwith give written notice to the Company identifying that person or group of connected persons and the Company shall be entitled to terminate this agreement by giving not less than two months' written notice to the Distributor within 28 days after the notice from the Distributor was given to the Company.

Termination shall be without prejudice to any right or remedy either party shall have arising prior to termination.

Any waiver by one of the parties of a breach of any provision of this agreement committed by the other party shall not be considered as a waiver of any subsequent breach of the same or any of the provisions.

Upon termination of this agreement the Company may repurchase from the Distributor any stocks of Products held by the Distributor at purchase price, provided that the Distributor may sell such products for which the Distributor has accepted orders from customers prior to the date of termination.

2. 中译英

第二十六条　有限责任公司的注册资本为在公司登记机关登记的全体股东认缴的出资额。法律、行政法规以及国务院决定对有限责任公司注册资本实缴、注册资本最低限额另有规定的，从其规定。

第二十七条　股东可以用货币出资，也可以用实物、知识产权、土地使用权等可以用货币估价并可以依法转让的非货币财产作价出资；但是，法律、行政法规规定不得作为出资的财产除外。对作为出资的非货币财产应当评估作价，核实财产，不得高估或者低估作价。法律、行政法规对评估作价有规定的，从其规定。

第二十八条　股东应当按期足额缴纳公司章程中规定的各自所认缴的出资额。股东以货币出资的，应当将货币出资足额存入有限责任公司在银行开设的账户；以非货币财产出资的，应当依法办理其财产权的转移手续。股东不按照前款规定缴纳出资的，除应当向公司足额缴纳外，还应当向已按期足额缴纳出资的股东承担违约责任。

第八单元　礼仪文书

第一模块：礼仪文书翻译概述

礼仪文书是为实现礼仪目的或在礼仪场合使用的文书，可以分为交往类文书（如通知、感谢信、致歉信、欢迎词、答谢词等）、聘邀类文书（如聘书、请柬等）、庆贺类文书（如书面庆典致辞等）和哀悼类文书（如吊唁、挽联等）。不管是哪类礼仪文书，基本都具备以下特点：社交性、礼节性和规范性等。正是因为这些特点，礼仪文书用词要力求准确、简洁、庄重，语法正确，所涉及的数字精确无误，句子长短适中。整体上遵守一些程式，使用一定的套语，做到礼貌得体、周到清晰、文雅又不失自尊。翻译礼仪文书时当然需要注意以上所述的各种文体特点，当然也要注意中英文礼仪文书的差异。

一、英文礼仪文书的文体特点及其翻译

（一）用词特点

英语礼仪文书用词首先要正式。具体说来，英语礼仪文书多用书面语、敬语等，充分体现了礼仪文书的规范正式、公事公办等特点，翻译时也要注意使用汉语正式的表达。以下表格中列出了日常词汇与礼仪文书常用词的区别及其汉语译文：

日常用词	礼仪文书用词	中文
about	in connection with/in view of	关于……
according to	as per/in accordance with	依据……
before	in advance of/prior to	先于……，在……之前
copy	duplicate	副本
or	otherwise	否则
send	dispatch	发送
so	therefore	因此
tell	inform/advise	告知，通知

英语礼仪文书与合同一样，也常使用here、there和where加上after、by、under、to、with、from、in等组成的复合副词，如hereafter、hereby、hereinafter、herewith、thereafter、thereby、therefrom、wherein、whereby等，显得严肃、庄重，翻译时注意中文表达也要正式、严谨。例如：

例1

A supply of these order forms is sent *herewith*.

随函附上一些订货单。

例2

Enclosed please find the quotation sheet. All offers and sales are subject to the terms and conditions printed on the reverse side *hereof*.

随函附上报价单，所有报盘与销售均应以本报价单背面所印条件为准。

例3

Notice is *hereby* given that the power supply is not available from 7:00 to 17:00 tomorrow, owing to the annual overhaul of the electrics.

由于年度电路大检修，明天7点至17点停电，特此通知。

英语礼仪文书中还经常使用一些礼貌用语。除英语中常用的礼貌词please外，还会使用welcome和appreciate这样的动词以及sincerely、faithfully、kindly、cordially、respectfully、unfortunately 等副词，传达请求、赞扬、尊重等感情。请看下面的例子：

例4

We would much *appreciate* a letter informing us of the result of your enquiries.
敬请来函告知贵方询盘结果。

例5

You are *welcome* to contact us in case of any petroleum related issue and it will be our pleasure to support you & company with professional expertise and knowledge.
如遇任何与石油相关的问题，<u>欢迎</u>联系我们。我方将很高兴为贵公司提供专业技术与知识。

例6

In reply to your enquiry of June 7, 2022, I *respectfully* offer my latest quotation herewith.
兹回复贵方2022年6月7日来函，特随函奉上我方最新报价。

涉及商务合作的礼仪文书中会出现一些专业词汇，甚至是专业缩略语。如pro forma invoice（形式发票）、quotation（报价）、counter-offer（还盘）、A/C No.（account number，账号）、A/Cs Rec.（accounts receivable，应收账款）、B/L（bill of lading，提货单）、CIF（cost, insurance and freight，到岸价）、D/P（documents against payment，付款交单）、FPA（free from particular average，平安险）、forex（foreign exchange，外汇）、L/C（letter of credit，信用证）等等。有关专业词汇和专业缩略语需要译者翻译时查阅相关资料，找到准确的中文对应表达，切不可妄加猜测。

（二）句式特点和语气特点

英语礼仪文书的句式特点与要表达的语气息息相关，所以这里将句式特点和语气特点一并分析讲解。

首先，英语礼仪文书中句式结构完整，符合规范，表达庄重的语气，译文要注意保留原文的语气。请看下面的例子：

例7

Mr. and Mrs. Oliver Barrett request the pleasure of your company at a dinner in celebration of Mr. Barrett's sixtieth birthday, Saturday, the sixth of March, at seven o'clock.
兹定于3月6日（星期六）晚七点设宴庆贺巴雷特先生六十寿辰，恭请光临。

八

例8

With the increase of the prices which becomes conspicuous this year, the next consignment will be much dearer, so we recommend you to take prompt advantage of this offer.

随着今年价格明显上涨，下一批货品价格会更高，因此建议贵方尽早利用本次报价。

以上两个例子一个出自邀请函，一个出自报价函，句子结构都非常完整，显得比较正式。中译文也忠实再现了原文的语气。

英语礼仪文书多用肯定句，少用否定句，旨在表现出友好礼貌的语气，或者使语气更加委婉、客气。请看下面的例子：

例9

If I understood your letter correctly, I would immediately accept your offer.

例9使用了虚拟语气，实际要表达的意思是：Your letter is not clear and I cannot understand it。很显然，这样表达显得粗鲁、直接，很容易伤害双方的关系，因此需要用肯定句委婉地表达出来。这样的句子如果直接翻译成"如果我能正确理解贵方函件，就会立刻接受报价"，会显得生硬，不如译成：

烦请来函更清楚些，以便我能立刻接受贵方报价。

例10

We shall be glad to fill your order as soon as we receive your check.

例10要表达的意思是We cannot fill your order because you have failed to send your check，但显然这种属于不礼貌、不委婉的表达。翻译如下：

烦请/恳请尽快寄来支票，以便我方填写贵方订单。

以上两个例子的译文表明，对上述英语中用来表达否定意义的肯定句，中译文完全可以做到保留原文礼貌、客气、委婉的语气。

英语礼仪文书中较少用祈使句，多用陈述句。我们知道，大多数的礼仪文书旨在邀请、请求或希望对方采取一定的行动，但祈使句透露着命令的语气，不够礼貌，而且显得不够正式。所以，礼仪文书中往往使用陈述句表示自己的愿望，使表达的语气委婉，有利于促成对方采取一定的行动。但翻译成汉语时，可以使用祈使句，不过需要借助谦词和敬词来显示措辞的礼貌，如"敬请""烦请""为盼"等。请看下面的例子：

例11

You are kindly requested to provide us with all possible information on your market.

烦请告知贵方市场详情。

例12

Your priority to the consideration of the above request will be appreciated.

敬请优先考虑上述请求。

例11实际要表达的意思是Please provide us with all possible information on your market，例12的意思是Please consider the above request。但是，英语中please使用频繁，这样的祈使句会让人感觉口语化，而且不礼貌，也不庄重。因此，礼仪文书中使用陈述句就不足为奇了。另外，正是由于要使用陈述句而非祈使句，所以英语中这类文体也常用被动语态，但翻译时基本转译为汉语的主动语态（例11和例12的译文均使用主动语态）。

英语礼仪文书中还常用一些套语，如告知不利于对方的消息时使用much to our regret、I'm sorry to tell ...、I regret to say ...、I appreciate sth. but ...、I'm afraid to ...等；告知有利于对方的消息时使用much to our delight、It's a pleasure for me to ...、I would like to inform ...等句型。这些句型翻译时基本都可以直译，如“遗憾地通知贵方”“虽然我很愿意……，但……”“很高兴通知贵方”等等，这里就不再举例赘述。

此外，还要注意英语礼仪文书中常用情态动词和虚拟语气来表达感激、愿望等，翻译时只要符合汉语的表达习惯即可。请看下面的例子：

例13

On behalf of our company, I *would like to extend* our best wishes on your marriage to Peter Leo.

欣闻你和彼得·利奥喜结连理，我谨代表公司向你表达最诚挚的祝福。

例14

I *should be grateful* if you will consider my application.

恳请考虑我的申请。

例15

Your information *would be appreciated* as to the discount for an order of 8,000 pairs of the leather shoes.

敬请告知订购8,000双皮鞋的折扣。

以上三个例子中would like to extend（例13）和should be grateful（例14）运用情态动词表达正式的语气，例15通过虚拟语气表达请求。由于汉语没有动词形式的变化，所以这些表达无法直接翻译，要根据具体意思进行调整。像例13只需要注重语气的正式，例14和例15就使用了“恳请”“敬请”这样的礼貌用语。

二、中文礼仪文书的文体特点及其翻译

（一）用词特点

中文礼仪文书用词一般较庄重，多使用文言词语，如“兹”“获悉”“收悉”“承蒙”“事宜”“均”“本函”“鉴于”“兹附上”“随函附上”等。这些庄重的文言表达不一定在英文中有对应词，可以考虑表达时运用英语中比较正式的词汇和古体词。请看下面的例子：

例16

贵方6月12日来函收悉，兹寄去面额为1500美元的支票一张，谨此奉复。

I am writing to inform you that we have received your letter of June 12. Enclosed please find a check of US$1,500.

例17

鉴于贵方违约造成我方不应有的损失，我方很遗憾地撤销此约，并保留对我方损失的索赔权。

In view of the fact that your violation of the contract has caused us undeserved losses, we regret to say that we have canceled the contract and we reserve the right to claim damages.

以上两个例子原文分别使用了“收悉”“兹”“谨此奉复”“鉴于”“此约”等，这些词在英语中没有对应的古体词，但是英语译文选择了一些正式用词，再现了原文的语气。

中文礼仪文书还倾向使用礼貌用语，其中最常用的是“贵公司/贵方/贵厂”“敬希”“敬请”“敬悉”“恭请”“烦请”“欣逢”“欣闻”等。这些都表明中国不愧于“礼仪之邦”的称号。请看下面的例子：

例18

欣闻母校百年华诞，特致函向母校致以热烈的祝贺！祝母校日新月异，兴旺发达，桃李芬芳。

I'm writing to extend my warmest congratulations on my alma mater's centenary. May she make progress with each passing day and thrive with more and more talent.

例19

2023年4月20日第十三届中国西部国际物流产业博览会将在西安举行，恭请莅临。

We sincerely welcome you to be present at the 13th Western China International Logistics Industry Expo to be held in Xi'an on April 20, 2023.

中文礼仪文书中也会使用一些专业词汇，特别是涉及商务往来的礼仪文书，例如"实盘"(firm offer)、"虚盘"(non-firm offer)、"保兑"(confirmation)、"运费"(freight charges)、"特惠税率"(preferential tariff)等。这些专业词汇翻译时需要在英语中找到对应的专业表达，此不赘述。

（二）句式特点

中文礼仪文书的句式特点首先在于多用祈使句，这些祈使句多用"敬请""恳请""烦请"等字样开头，译成英文时要注意前文提及的英文礼仪文书的句式特点，尽量使用陈述句，而非直译为英语的祈使句。请看下面的例子：

例20

敬请立刻修改信用证以便我方及时发货。

We should be obliged for your immediate amendment of the L/C to enable us to make timely shipment.

例21

请允许我代表公司来函对史密斯即将到访我司表示由衷的欢迎。

I am writing on behalf of my company to extend our warmest welcome to Mr. Smith for his visit to our company.

以上两个例子原文属于祈使句，英文均译为了陈述句，语气正式，符合前文讲述的英语礼仪文书的特点。

中文礼仪文书还多用无主句，表达希望、建议等。为了表达礼貌和客观的语气，建议这类句子英译时使用被动语态。例如：

例22

特奉上我公司例行调查表格一份，希望贵处妥为填写寄还。

A copy of our routine survey form is enclosed herewith, and it is hoped that you will fill it in and return it properly.

例23

建议贵方派技术人员到我方就技术细节进行磋商。

It is hereby recommended that you send technicians to have a discussion with us on technical details.

以上两个例子的译文均使用了被动语态，而且添加了古体词herewith和hereby，再现了原文礼貌、正式、庄重的语气。

中文礼仪文书中有些句子较长，里面含有多个小分句。译成英语时，可以考虑适当拆句，因为英语的礼仪文书句子不是很长。请看下面的例子：

例24

我司从中国驻贵国大使馆商务参赞处获悉贵公司是信誉卓著的轻工产品进口商，我公司以经营轻工产品为主，现寄去商品目录和价目单，用以向贵公司毛遂自荐。

We learned from the Commercial Counselor's Office of the Embassy of the People's Republic of China to your country that you are a prestigious light industrial products importer, which has made us eager to enter into business relations with you. Accordingly, we, as a corporation dealing exclusively in light industrial products, hereby introduce ourselves to you by sending you our catalogs and price-lists.

例25

我们即将告别成绩斐然的2022年，迎来充满希望的2023年，在此我谨代表公司总经办向全体员工的努力进取和勤奋工作致以深深的谢意，祝大家在新的一年里和气致祥，身体健康，家庭康泰，万事如意！

We are saying goodbye to the fruitful year of 2022 and welcoming the hopeful 2023. I would like to take this opportunity to extend the heartfelt gratitude on behalf of the Office of the General Manager to all of you for your hard work. All the best wishes to you and your family. May you be healthy and lucky in the new year.

例24和例25原文句子都比较长，但因为有多个小分句组成，汉语读起来并不显得冗长，如果在英文里译成一句话就会显得太长，不符合英语礼仪文书的特点，因此需要拆分。

三、礼仪文书翻译原则与策略归纳

综合前面的讲解，可以将礼仪文书翻译的原则归纳如下：(1) 礼仪文书的译文格式应正确。中英文礼仪文书都有自己的格式规范，译文要符合目的语的格式规范。(2) 用词恰当。中英文礼仪文书都会使用专业词汇、正式表达和语气庄重的词汇，所以需要在目的语中用恰当的词汇再现出来。(3) 句法和句式规范。中英文礼仪文书在句法和句式方面都有自己的特点，因此表达要规范。(4) 注重细节，语气贴切。礼仪文书在语气方面有自己的特点，有些商务往来的礼仪文书还包含数字，因此翻译时要注重这些细节，同时注意把握礼仪文书的语气，特别是礼貌、委婉的语气。礼仪文书的具体翻译策略可归纳为下表：

英译中

	英文礼仪文书的文体特点	翻译策略
词汇	使用正式词汇。	中文对应词汇也要正式。
	常使用一些here和there加介词的古体词。	中文可以选用一些文言词汇，不一定与这些词对应，可以在句子的其他地方使用文言词汇。
	常使用相关内容和主题的专业词汇。	中文也选用对应的专业词汇。
句式	句式结构完整	中文基本要忠实地译出原文的结构。
	多用肯定句，少用否定句。	根据中文礼仪文书的表达习惯翻译。
	多用陈述句，少用祈使句。	中文基本使用祈使句，但开头可用“烦请”“恳请”等字样。
	虚拟语气	根据中文表达习惯再现语气。

中译英

	中文礼仪文书的文体特点	翻译策略
词汇	常使用文言词汇。	可选用英语的古体词。
	常使用相关内容和主题的专业词汇。	使用英语对应的专业词汇。

（待续）

（续表）

	中文礼仪文书的文体特点	翻译策略
句式	常使用带有“请”“烦请”“敬请”等开头的祈使句。	英语用比较正式的陈述句。
	常使用无主句表示建议和希望。	使用英语被动句。
	常用一些长句。	拆分成多个英语句子。

八

第二模块：英文礼仪文书语篇汉译解析

原文

Nov. 11, 2019

Dear Mr. Li,

We are considering providing each of our sales representatives with a pocket calculator. We saw your Model AMB displayed at China Import and Export Fair last month and found that it would meet our needs very well.

We know that AMB costs US$36.2 each, but we wonder whether there is a trade discount for fairly large quantities. Our first order will be 200.

Besides the price information, we also need complete details about your services, warranties, carrying case, battery—any information that may help us in making the purchase decision.

Your prompt reply would be appreciated.

Cordially yours,

Max Wolf

Deputy Manager

翻译解析

本篇是礼仪文书中的商务信函，属于公函。当今社会，公函可以是纸质版，也可以是电子版，甚至是邮件往来。公函是一种特别常见的礼仪文书。翻译这类文书时除了注意如何传达文体特色外，还需要注意格式。具体解析如下。

1. 公函格式

中英文信函的格式基本相同，但也有不同之处。比如，英语信函的日期是写在前面，中文的日期写在最后，所以翻译时要作出调整。英语信函落款处先写写信人的姓名，再写职位；中文一般先写职务再写姓名，或者将职务放在括号内，所以也需要进行调整。英语公函的最后Cordially yours可以不译，但要根据中文公函的习惯写上“此致”“敬礼”的字样。上述调整请参考后面的译文。

2. 公函称谓

英文公函开头的称谓有两种。收信人明确的，就使用Dear ××，不明确的用Dear Sir/Madam。前一种要译为“尊敬的某某”，而不是“亲爱的某某”，后一种则译为“敬启者”。此外，可以在称谓下面按照中文公函的习惯加上“您好”二字，具体可参考后面的译文。

3. 暗含“请求”的陈述句

本函中最后一句话（Your prompt reply would be appreciated）是陈述句，而且使用了虚拟语气和被动语态，实际上是请对方尽快回复，根据中文信函的习惯，可译为“敬请回复”。

4. 措辞

本篇的中文译文要使用比较正式的措辞。请看下面几句话的翻译：

（1）We are considering providing each of our sales representatives with a pocket calculator.

这里的we最好翻译成“我司”，显得比较正式。整句话拟译如下：

我司正在考虑为每位销售代表配备一台袖珍计算器。

（2）We saw your Model AMB displayed at China Import and Export Fair last month and found that it would meet our needs very well.

这里的your Model AMB可译为“贵方的AMB型”，后面还可以使用“该款计算器”。整句话拟译为：

我们在上月举行的广交会上看到贵方展出的AMB型，认为该款计算器能满足我方要求。

（3）We know that AMB costs US$36.2 each, but we wonder whether there is a trade discount for fairly large quantities.

这里的we wonder表示一种商量的语气，不要直接译为“我们想知道”。整句话拟译如下：

据我方所知，AMB每台售价36.2美元，不知大批订购是否另有优惠。

八 参考译文

尊敬的李先生：

您好！

我司正在考虑为每位销售代表配备一台袖珍计算器。我们在上月举行的广交会上看到贵方展出的AMB型，认为该款计算器能满足我方要求。

据我方所知，AMB每台售价36.2美元，不知大批订购是否另有优惠。我方首批订货将为200台。

除价格信息外，我方还想了解有关贵方服务、保修、携带护套、电池等细节，即有助于我方做出购买决定的任何信息。

敬请回复。

此致

敬礼！

马克斯·沃尔夫（Max Wolf）

（公司副经理）

2019年11月11日

第三模块：中文礼仪文书语篇英译解析

原文

贺信

欣闻××泥塑艺术协会成立，倍感欣慰和自豪，特致贺信，表示衷心祝贺。

中国泥塑艺术依据民俗而生，顺应时代而变。××泥塑艺术协会的成立顺应了时代要求，必将吸引众人的目光。该协会的成立有助于中国泥塑艺术的传承与保护，中国泥塑艺术的明天会更加辉煌，永远俏立于民间艺术之林。

预祝××泥塑艺术协会成立大会取得圆满成功！祝愿中国民间艺术的明天更辉煌！

××艺术学院院长
李××
2021年5月16日

翻译解析

本篇属于贺信，是礼仪文书的一种。本篇翻译时要注意一些格式调整和措辞表达。

1. 格式调整

翻译本篇时，需要注意时间位置的调整，由中文的最后调到英文的题目之后；“××艺术学院院长李××”需要把人名放在前面，换行后再翻译职位，具体调整请参见后面的译文。

2. 无主句

本篇第一段“欣闻××泥塑艺术协会成立，倍感欣慰和自豪，特致贺信，表示衷心祝贺”属于无主句，也是中文贺信常用的格式，翻译时可添加主语I。另外，该句语气渲染性较强，英语译文无法完全传达出来，要按照英语的表达习惯适当删减。整句话可拆译为两个英语句子，拟译如下：

I am writing to extend our sincere congratulations on the founding of ×× Clay Sculpture Art Society. It is really something that we feel proud of.

3. 长句

本篇有一个长句，可以对应译为一句。具体如下：

该协会的成立有助于中国泥塑艺术的传承与保护，中国泥塑艺术的明天会更加辉煌，永远俏立于民间艺术之林。

这里的主语“该协会的成立”与前面一句的主语相同，所以此处可以直接用it做主语，主结构是第一个小分句，后面的部分可以考虑用定语从句。拟译如下：

It will contribute to the passing-down and protection of China’s clay sculpture art, which will enjoy a better future as one of the folk art forms.

4. 祝福语

最后一段是祝福语，可以选择英语常用的祝福套语进行翻译，一种是wish sb. sth.，一种是may ... do。所以可以有以下两种译法：

（1）I wish the inaugural meeting of ×× Clay Sculpture Art Society a great success and China's folk art a brilliant future.

（2）May the inaugural meeting of ×× Clay Sculpture Art Society be a great success. May China's folk art have a brilliant future.

八

参考译文

Letter of Congratulations

May 16, 2021

I am writing to extend our sincere congratulations on the founding of ×× Clay Sculpture Art Society. It is really something that we feel proud of.

China's clay sculpture has its root in folklore and changes with times. The founding of ×× Clay Sculpture Art Society conforms to the trend of the times, so it will attract the attention of the public. It will contribute to the passing-down and protection of China's clay sculpture art, which will enjoy a better future as one of the folk art forms.

May the inaugural meeting of ×× Clay Sculpture Art Society be a great success. May China's folk art have a brilliant future.

Li ××

Dean of ×× Academy of Arts

第四模块：翻译练习

1. 英译中

Dec. 16, 2020

Dear Mr. Li,

You will remember that last month we ordered 24 Tanson 1 GHz Pentium X Computers. When we discussed delivery dates, you assured us that you could deliver by December 2nd. However, the goods are now two weeks overdue, and I have heard nothing from you to confirm a definite delivery date.

We urgently need these computers to upgrade the administrative functioning of our offices, and your slowness is causing a great deal of inconvenience.

I should appreciate your looking into this matter and arranging for delivery of these computers within the next three days. I am afraid that if you are unable to deliver the computers within this period, we shall be compelled to cancel our order and purchase from another supplier.

Yours sincerely,
Kadir Aboe
Office Manager

2. 中译英

尊敬的帕克先生：

您好！

我们对B&G公司的访问即将结束，马上启程回到北京。

在我们离别之际，我谨代表本公司向贵方在我们逗留期间提供的热情款待表示衷心的感谢。我们都认为此次访问取得了圆满成功，相信此次访问会有助于进一步加强双方的业务合作。

衷心希望贵方尽早来北京参观访问，从而给予我方机会报答贵方的热情款待。我的同事和我将非常愿意在不久的将来能够宴请您和您的同事。届时，我们还可以就双方更密切的合作进行磋商，从而扩大双方的业务往来。

最后，祝您身体健康，工作顺利！

此致

敬礼！

××公司销售经理
王利
2020年7月20日

第九单元　政府与组织文件

第一模块：政府与组织文件翻译概述

政府与组织文件的翻译是一种非常重要的应用翻译。政府文件指的是一国政府发布的有关政治、经济、外交等方面的文件，组织文件指的是政府之外其他组织机构发布的各种文件。这些文件属于信息类文本，在文体方面具有公文的性质。英文文件一般句子比较长，名词短语使用频繁；中文文件会出现一些中国特色的词汇，句子也比较长，但动词使用频繁。中英文的政府和组织文件整体风格偏于正式。下面分别探讨英文政府与组织文件和中文政府与组织文件的文体特点和翻译。

一、英文政府与组织文件的文体特点及其翻译

（一）用词特点

英语政府与组织文件的用词一般比较正式，显示这些文件的严肃性。请看下面的例子：

例1

The Federal Government benefits from a professional cadre of administrative law judges appointed under section 3105 of title 5, United States Code (USC), who are impartial and committed to the rule of law.

行政法官遵照《美国法典》第五编第3105节进行任命，这是一支秉持公正、法治原则的专业行政法官队伍，对联邦政府发挥着重要作用。

例2

Wide variations in the quality and security of forms of identification used to gain access to secure Federal and other facilities where there is potential for terrorist attacks need to be eliminated.

一些联邦设施及其他设施属于安全设施，可能遭到恐怖袭击，目前进入这些设施所使用的身份证明形式不一，在质量和安全方面参差不齐，这些差异亟待消除。

例3

The problem of population control has to be recognized and approached in a world environmental context.

须联系世界环境去认识和解决人口控制问题。

以上三个例句原文均使用了比较正式的词汇，如例1中的under和committed，例2中的gain access to，例3中的recognize和approach，译文也设法让措辞比较正式，如使用了"遵照""亟待""须"等，以保证传达原文正式的语气。

英语政府与组织文件名词使用比较频繁，主要是由动词或形容词加后缀构成的名词，使用名词是因为句子中语法功能的需要，实际上其动词的意义仍然十分明显，一般用介词短语引出其逻辑上的主语或宾语，因此，翻译时尽量转译为汉语的动词才能使得译文更加通顺。请看下面的例子：

例4

These include *enforcement* of a ban on new construction of CFC-11 foam production facilities, production *control* of CFC-11, and export and import *control* of ODS.

这些措施包括实施新建氟利昂-11（CFC-11）发泡剂生产设施的禁令、控制其产量以及控制消耗臭氧层物质（ODS）进出口。

例5

These include strong government *ownership* of education sector policies, *channeling* of aid into government sector budgets, *reduction* of duplication of effort and *carrying out* of joint field missions, joint *analytic work* and mutual progress *assessments*.

这些原则包括政府有力地掌控教育部门的政策，将援助纳入政府部门的预算，减少重复性工作，共同开展实地考察，共同分析，共同评估进展情况。

例6

Violence against women has been tackled through legislative measures including the new laws on domestic violence and *trafficking* and *exploitation* of women, the *setting up* of new mechanisms for the *protection* and *support* of victims and the *training* of professionals, particularly police officers, involved in the *handling* of violence cases.

针对妇女的暴力问题采取了一系列措施进行解决，首先是设立新法惩治家庭暴力，禁止<u>贩卖</u>妇女与<u>剥夺</u>妇女权利；其次是<u>建立保护</u>和<u>支持</u>受害者的新机制；第三是<u>培训</u>专业人员，特别是<u>处理</u>妇女暴力案件的警官。

以上三个例子中，原文斜体的单词或词组均为名词，但基本上都包含动作意义，如果直接将这些词译为名词，翻译腔比较重，不如将它们译成动词，汉语读起来也非常通顺。

（二）句式特点

政府与组织文件属于信息类文本，大多数时候语气比较客观，风格比较正式，因此英语句子中常用被动语态。这些被动语态译成中文时往往要转译为主动语态。请看下面的例子：

例7

Other organs/bodies/committees/structures have been put in place in the public sector during the period under review promoting gender equality according to their specific sphere of competence.

评估期间，公共部门中其他机关/实体/委员会/机构也都行动起来，根据本机构的具体职能致力于促进男女平等。

例8

In addition, reports concerning investigation of each individual complaint are submitted to the competent public service department/officer, and contain, in the event of the finding of violation, the ombudsman's suggestions or recommendations for reparation measures within specified period.

另外，还要向职能公共服务部门/官员提交每个投诉的调查报告，里面含调查员的建议，即若发现侵权的情况，在一定时间内需采取何种弥补措施。

例9

The setting up of an Equal Opportunities Commission to investigate complaints of sex-discrimination has been extensively discussed during these years.

近年来，对成立平等机会委员会以调查性别歧视投诉进行了广泛的讨论。

以上三个例子均含有被动语态，也全都转译成了汉语的主动语态，例7的译文基本没有改变原文的顺序，例8和例9则转译为无主句。

政府与组织文件既然是信息类文本，很多信息需要用一句话说完，因此，英语中此类文本的长句使用频繁，这些长句中往往包含定语从句，大多为补充说明性质的非限定性定语从句。非限定性定语从句可处理为独立的小分句，不必放在被修饰词前做定语。请看下面的例子：

例10

The National Machinery for Women's Rights (NMWR) plays a key role in the formulation, coordination and implementation of the government's policy in this field, in collaboration with NGOs and all sectoral ministries, which remain primarily responsible for the implementation of gender equality policies within their own sphere of competence.

妇女权利国家机制（NMWR）与非政府组织和所有部门合作，在本领域的政府政策制定、协调和实施方面起着重要作用。各部门主要负责实施其职能范围内的男女平等政策。

该例以非限定性定语从句结尾，翻译时可先不考虑该从句，将其译为独立的句子放在译文的最后。这样一来，该句的翻译就简单多了。

例11

In addition, some of those who are considered literate but cannot read or understand English, which is the primary medium of communication used by most human rights advocates in the country, cannot understand the human rights issues properly.

另外，被认为有文化但读不懂英语或听不懂英语的人也无法正确理解人权问题，而英语是该国大多数人权宣传使用的基本交际工具。

该例有两个定语从句，一个是限定性定语从句who are considered literate but cannot read or understand English，另一个是非限定性定语从句which is the primary medium of communication used by most human rights advocates in the country。限定性定语从句可以译为中文的定语，非限定性定语从句如果还放在原来的位置，中文读起来有点拗口，所以将它调整至译文最后。

二、中文政府与组织文件的文体特点及其翻译

（一）用词特点

中文政府与组织文件用词和英语一样，也相对正式，偏文雅。翻译时需要注意英语尽可能使用一些正式词汇，从而传达原文正式的语气。请看下面的例子：

例12

我们重申致力于工业领域合作，包括产能和产业政策、新型工业基础设施与标准、中小微企业等，共同抓住新工业革命带来的机遇，加速金砖国家工业化进程。

We reaffirm our commitment to BRICS industrial cooperation in industrial capacities and policies, new industrial infrastructure and standards, and among micro, small and medium-sized enterprises, to jointly seize the opportunities brought about by the new industrial revolution and expedite our respective industrialization.

例13

实践证明，"一带一路"倡议顺应时代潮流，符合各国人民利益，为推动构建人类命运共同体提供了实践平台。

Practice has proven that the Belt and Road Initiative conforms to the trend of the times, serves the interests of people of all countries, and provides a platform for the building of a community of shared future for humankind.

例14

全球疫情防控战，已经成为维护全球公共卫生安全之战、维护人类健康福祉之战、维护世界繁荣发展之战、维护国际道义良知之战，事关人类前途命运。人类唯有战而胜之，别无他路。

Preventing and controlling the spread of the virus has become a fight to safeguard global public health, to secure the wellbeing of humanity, to maintain the world prosperity, and to enforce morality and conscience on the international community. It is a fight that will determine the future of the human race. We have no other choice but to overcome the pandemic.

以上三个例子的原文用词都比较正式，英文在选词方面也要正式，少用俚语和口语表达。

中文政府文件中常出现中国特色的词汇，有的还是一些缩略表达，翻译时应将意思传达清楚和准确，保证英语读者明白其中的意思，从而更好地讲好中国故事。请看下面的例子：

例15

严格落实中央八项规定精神，持之以恒纠治“四风”，重点纠治形式主义、官僚主义，“三公”经费大幅压减。

We strictly complied with the central Party leadership's eight-point decision on improving work conduct and kept up our efforts to tackle pointless formalities, bureaucratism, hedonism, and extravagance, with emphasis on the first two. Spending on official overseas visits, vehicles for official use, and official hospitality was slashed.

这里的“四风”和“三公”属于中国特色词汇，而且是缩略表达，翻译时建议将具体意思翻译出来。“四风”指“形式主义、官僚主义、享乐主义和奢靡之风”，所以译为pointless formalities, bureaucratism, hedonism, and extravagance，“三公”指“因公出国（境）、公务车购置及运行、公务招待”，所以译为official overseas visits, vehicles for official use, and official hospitality。

例16

各地区各部门坚持以习近平新时代中国特色社会主义思想为指导，深刻领悟“两个确立”的决定性意义，增强“四个意识”、坚定“四个自信”、做到“两个维护”。

All localities and government departments followed the guidance of Xi Jinping Thought on Socialism with Chinese Characteristics for a New Era; gained a deep understanding of the decisive significance of affirming Comrade Xi Jinping's core position on the Party Central Committee and in the Party as a whole and affirming the guiding role of Xi Jinping Thought on Socialism with Chinese Characteristics for a New Era; enhanced their consciousness of the need to maintain political integrity, think in big-picture terms, follow the leadership core, and keep in alignment with the central Party leadership; stayed confident in the path, theory, system, and culture of socialism with Chinese characteristics; upheld Comrade Xi Jinping's core position on the Party Central Committee and in the Party as a whole and upheld the Central Committee's authority and its centralized, unified leadership.

该例中“两个确立”指党确立习近平同志党中央的核心、全党的核心地位，确立习近平新时代中国特色社会主义思想的指导地位；“四个意识”指政治意识、大局意识、核心意识和看齐意识；“四个自信”指道路自信、理论自信、制度自信、文化自信；“两个维护”指坚决维护习近平总书记党中央的核心、全党的核心地位，坚决维护党中央权威和集中统一领导。这几个概念在翻译时需要进行解释说明，将具体内涵译出，英语读者才能明白其中的意思。

任何语言表达均离不开其背后的思维模式。中文背后是中国人的审美和艺术思维，因此，中文政府文件中会使用一些渲染语气的词汇，如一些形容词或副词以及重复性的四字格。这些渲染语气的词汇翻译时需要低调处理，有时候还需要省译，尤其是前后重复的四字格一般仅译出意思，避免译文出现词语堆砌的情况。请看下面的例子：

例17

中国把人民生命安全和身体健康放在第一位，以坚定果敢的勇气和决心，采取最全面最严格最彻底的防控措施，有效阻断病毒传播链条。14亿中国人民坚韧奉献、团结协作，构筑起同心战疫的坚固防线，彰显了人民的伟大力量。

Making people's lives and health its first priority, China adopted extensive, stringent, and thorough containment measures, and has for now succeeded in cutting all channels for the transmission of the virus. 1.4 billion Chinese people have exhibited *tenacity* and *solidarity* in erecting a defensive rampart that demonstrates their *strength* in the face of such natural disasters.

该例中“团结协作”里的“团结”和“协作”是同一个意思，所以仅译为solidarity即可。“坚韧奉献”中的“奉献”和“伟大力量”中的“伟大”属于中文渲染语气的词，英文中省译，分别译为tenacity和strength。如果按照中文逐字翻译，译文会显得冗余，不利于英语读者理解。

例18

坚持尽力而为、量力而行，不断提升公共服务水平，着力解决人民群众普遍关心关注的民生问题。

We will *do everything within our capacity* to keep enhancing public services and resolve issues that are of common concern to the people.

该例中的“尽力而为”和“量力而行”表达相同的含义，可合并翻译为do everything within our capacity。此外，“着力”表示“尽力，用力”，是政府文件中经常使用的渲染词，英译时可以省略。

（二）句式特点

中文政府和组织文件也属于信息文本，常使用无主句来表示政府机构要做什么，不要做什么，或者号召人民一起做什么，不做什么。这些无主句翻译时大多需要添加主语we，个别情况下也可使用被动语态。请看下面的例子：

例19

坚持和完善社会主义基本经济制度，毫不动摇巩固和发展公有制经济，毫不动摇鼓励、支持、引导非公有制经济发展，充分发挥市场在资源配置中的决定性作用，更好发挥政府作用。

We must uphold and improve China's basic socialist economic systems. We must unswervingly consolidate and develop the public sector and unswervingly encourage, support, and guide the development of the non-public sector. We will work to see that the market plays the decisive role in resource allocation and that the government better plays its role.

该例是一个长句，没有主语，多个动宾短语构成的小分句并列。翻译时根据原文的语境，添加了主语we，有些地方使用一个动词，让宾语并列。因为动宾短语较多，所以在适当的地方进行了拆句处理。

例20

必须尽快提升安全防护能力水平，加强关键信息基础设施保护，加强网络安全信息统筹机制、手段、平台建设，加强网络安全事件应急指挥能力建设，积极发展网络安全产业，做到关口前移，防患于未然。

We must improve our capacity in cybersecurity protection as soon as possible, and strengthen information infrastructure security protection, and construction of the mechanism, means and platforms for cybersecurity information coordination. We must build the capacity in guiding cybersecurity emergency response, develop cybersecurity industries, and prevent any hazards in advance.

例20和例19一样，也没有主语，多个动宾短语并列。翻译时可根据原文的语境添加主语we，来表示一种承诺和义务。由于动宾短语比较多，所以有些地方使用一个动词，让宾语并列。有些地方则拆句处理。

实际上，从上面的例子也可以看出，中文政府和组织文件中常用连动式，即多个动词并列。这些并列动词如果表达的是一个意思，英语译文使用一个动词译出即可，宾语并列。如果并列动词表达的意思并不相近，则应分别译为不同的英语动词，并根据这些动词短语之间的关系考虑使用一些分词或不定式短语，有的则需要拆句处理。以上是一些没有主语的动词短语连用，下面两个例子则是有主语的：

例21

中国一直致力于维护亚太地区的和平与稳定，坚持走和平发展道路，坚持互利共赢的开放战略，坚持在和平共处五项原则基础上同所有国家发展友好合作，全面参与区域合作，积极应对传统安全和非传统安全挑战，为推动建设持久和平、共同繁荣的亚太不懈努力。

China is committed to promoting peace and stability in the Asian-Pacific region. It follows the path of peaceful development and the mutually beneficial strategy of opening up, and pursues friendly cooperation with all countries on the basis of the Five Principles of Peaceful Coexistence. It has participated in regional cooperation in an all-round way and taken active steps in response to both traditional and non-traditional security challenges, contributing to lasting peace and common prosperity in the Asia-Pacific region.

该例中原文主语是“中国”，第一个小句总领下文，可单独译成一句。后面跟了一系列动词，可根据语义在“全面参与区域合作”之前断开，将三个“坚持”放在一起翻译。剩下的部分根据动词短语之间的关系，将最后的“为推动建设持久和平、共同繁荣的亚太不懈努力”译成现在分词结构。

例22

近一年来，中国持续强化关键信息基础设施保护，开展覆盖全国的关键信息基础设施网络安全检查，深入排查重点领域、重要行业关键信息基础设施的网络安全风险隐患，提高网络安全防护能力。

Over the past year, China has reinforced the protection of critical information infrastructure, carried out cybersecurity examinations of the infrastructure, and checked the risks of cybersecurity concerning such infrastructure of key areas and industries to enhance the capability of cybersecurity protection.

这句话的主语也是“中国”，后面跟了一系列动词，包括“强化”“开展”“排查”以及“提高”，仔细分析后会发现，“提高网络安全防护能力”是前面三个动词的目的，因此翻译时可以将前三个动词短语并列，后面译为不定式表示目的。

中文政府和组织文件中句子一般较长，用多个小分句连成一句话，是中文读者习惯的行文方式。但是，英语句子是主从结构，如果中文长句理不清关系就直译为英文长句，会让英语读者感觉一头雾水。所以，翻译该类长句时，一方面根据动词之间的关系，判断是译为并列短语结构，还是将部分动词译成分词短语或不定式；另一方面根据语义，判断是否可以拆译为多个英语句子。请看下面的例子：

例23

网络空间已成为中国亿万网民共同的精神家园，中国坚持正能量是总要求、管得住是硬道理，不断加强网上内容建设，持续开展“中国好网民”工程、“网络媒体新春走基层”活动，推出一批现象级新闻报道和主题宣传，进一步传播和弘扬社会主义核心价值观；网络优质内容供给能力不断提升，培育养成一大批数字内容消费群体。

The cyberspace is the common home of China's Internet users. Positive energy publicity is the general requirement, and controllability is the absolute principle. The country is enhancing content building, launching projects such as Good Internet Users in China and Network Media Reporting for the Grass Roots during the Spring Festival, as well as phenomenal news broadcasts and thematic publicity products, and introducing and spreading core socialist values. The capability of excellent cyber content supply keeps being enhanced, and communities of digital content consumers have been cultivated.

这个例子的原文有多个小分句，根据其中的意思拆分成了四个英语句子。其中第三个句子使用四个动词并列，均使用进行时，后面三个动词前可以省略is。

例24

深化人才发展体制机制改革，真心爱才、悉心育才、倾心引才、精心用才，求贤若渴，不拘一格，把各方面优秀人才集聚到党和人民事业中来。

We will further reform the systems and mechanisms for talent development and ensure we value talented people, nurture them, attract them, and put them to good use. No effort should be spared and no rigid boundaries drawn in the endeavor to bring together the best and the brightest from all fields for the cause of the Party and the people.

该例原文包含多个小分句，译文拆分为两句。“真心爱才、悉心育才、倾心引才、精心用才”和“深化人才发展体制机制改革”在语义上是前后关联的，所以可并列在一起。“把各方面优秀人才集聚到党和人民事业中来”是“求贤若渴，不拘一格”的目的，所以用动词不定式来翻译。

三、政府与组织文件翻译原则与策略归纳

综上所述，中英文政府和组织文件均属于信息类文本，同时也是公文的一种。因此，两种语言中此类文件均注重传达信息，语气正式。翻译时要遵循以下原则：（1）忠实传达原文的实质信息；（2）忠实再现原文的风格；（3）译文表达通顺、地道；（4）注意中英文此类文件在表达风格上的区别，如英语更倾向使用由动词或形容词转换成的名词，翻译时需要将这样的名词转译为动词；中文会使用一些渲染语气的词、中国特色表达或无主句、连动式等，翻译时要注意根据英语表达特点进行适当省译、给出注释、添加主语、调整结构等。两种语言中政府和组织文件的翻译策略可归纳为下表：

英译中

	英文政府与组织文件的文体特点	翻译策略
词汇	用词正式	中译文也使用正式词汇。
	由动词转换成的抽象名词使用频繁	一般要转译为汉语的动词。
句式	被动语态使用相对频繁	一般转译为汉语的主动语态。
	长句使用相对频繁，特别是句内经常使用非限定性定语从句表示补充说明。	厘清句内的逻辑关系，使用汉语的小分句，非限定性定语从句翻译时一般不用前置处理为定语成分，而是译为独立分句，表示补充说明。

中译英

	中文政府与组织文件的文体特点	翻译策略
词汇	一般使用正式词汇，特别是偏文言的词汇。	英译文也使用正式词汇。
	中国特色词汇使用频繁	传达清楚其中的意思，有时需要进行解释。
	使用渲染语气的词汇，彰显中国审美特色。	按照英语背后的思维模式进行低调处理，有些要省译。
句式	无主句使用频繁	译文中一般添加主语we，个别情况下可译为被动句。
	句子较长，含多个并列小分句，往往使用多个连动式，即动宾短语连用。	转译为英语的主从结构，使用一些短语；有时需要拆句，即译成多个英语句子。

第二模块：英文政府与组织文件语篇汉译解析

原文

The Education for All Development Index (EDI), introduced in 2003, provides a summary measure of a country's situation vis-à-vis EFA. It covers four goals: UPE, adult literacy, gender, and quality of education. The data are insufficiently standardized to allow inclusion of early childhood care and education and life skills. Each goal in the EDI has a proxy indicator: total net enrolment ratio for UPE, the literacy rate among persons age 15 and over for adult literacy, the gender-specific EFA index for gender and the survival rate to grade 5 for education quality. The EDI falls between 0 and 1, with 1 representing EFA achievement. The index for 2002 is computed for the 123 countries for which data are available on all four components. Results show that:

- Forty-six countries have an EDI above 0.95, and can thus be considered as having achieved EFA or being close to doing so. These countries are mostly located in North America and Europe, where education has been compulsory for decades.
- Forty-nine countries, in all regions, have EDI values between 0.80 and 0.94. Quality remains an issue especially in Latin America and the Caribbean. In the Arab States, low adult literacy rates pull the EDI down.
- Twenty-eight countries have EDI values below 0.80. More than half are in sub-Saharan Africa. In these countries, all four components of the EDI are at low levels. They are unlikely to achieve EFA by 2015 without dramatically stepped-up efforts, including international support, though there is very rapid and encouraging change among many of the countries with the lowest indicators.

翻译解析

本篇属于国际组织报告，介绍一些国家的教育指数，涉及有关教育的专业表达，还有一些被动句和长句。下面具体分析翻译需要注意的问题。

1. 专业术语

（1） adult literacy：成人扫盲

（2） net enrolment ratio：净入学率

（3） literacy rate：识字率

2. 缩略语

本篇含有一些缩略语，翻译时要注意传达其准确的意思，要根据上下文找到中文对应的表达。另外，缩略语在中文行文中尽量不要使用英语原文，而是使用中文的对应表达。

（1） Education for All Development Index (EDI)：全民教育发展指数

（2） EFA：全民教育（英语全称为Education for All）

（3） UPE：普及初等教育（英语全称为Universal Primary Education）

3. 被动语态

本篇有几处使用了被动语态，这也是政府与组织文件常见的现象。如本章所讲，英语被动语态大多需要转译为汉语的主动语态。

（1）The data are insufficiently standardized to allow inclusion of early childhood care and education and life skills.

这里的被动语态are insufficiently standardized显然不能译成“没有充分被标准化”，而应译成主动语态，即“不够标准”。整句话拟译为：

所使用的数据还不够标准，无法把儿童早期的培养和教育以及生活技能纳入其中。

（2）Forty-six countries have an EDI above 0.95, and can thus be considered as having achieved EFA or being close to doing so.

这里的can be considered as译为“可视为”比“可被视为”更通顺。整句话拟译为：

46个国家的全民教育发展指数大于0.95，因此可以视为这些国家已达到或接近于全民教育。

4. 定语从句

英语政府和组织文件中定语从句使用比较频繁，其中限定性定语从句要根据定语从句的长短以及所修饰的先行词是否还有其他修饰成分来决定翻译中如何处理，而非限定性定语从句翻译时最好就处理成小分句。

（1）The index for 2002 is computed for the 123 countries for which data are available on all four components.

这里的for which data are available on all four components本身就比较长，如果翻译成前置定语，句子会比较冗长。另外，通过语义分析可以看出，这个定语从句的内容是前面主结构的原因，因此，翻译时考虑将定语从句后置并添加表示原因的关联词。整句话拟译为：

2002年的指数基于123个国家的数据计算，因为从这些国家中能获得四个方面的数据。

（2）These countries are mostly located in North America and Europe, where education has been compulsory for decades.

这里的定语从句属于非限定性定语从句，所以翻译就简单多了，保留原文语序，将该从句放在译文的最后即可。整句话拟译为：

这些国家大部分位于北美洲和欧洲，几十年来一直实施义务教育。

5. 静态转译为动态

英语政府和组织文件中常使用一些由动词派生而来的名词，实际上带有很强的动词意义，翻译时应该考虑转译为中文的动词。请看下面一句：

The data are insufficiently standardized to allow inclusion of early childhood care and education and life skills.

这里的inclusion由include转化而来，后面的early childhood care and education and life skills实际上是其逻辑上的宾语，所以不如将这个名词译为动词，中文读起来更通顺。整句话拟译为：

所使用的数据还不够标准，无法把儿童早期的培养和教育以及生活技能纳入其中。

6. 长句

本篇有两个句子比较长，翻译时需要仔细分析，厘清逻辑关系，然后再转换为汉语。

（1）Each goal in the EDI has a proxy indicator: total net enrolment ratio for UPE, the literacy rate among persons age 15 and over for adult literacy, the gender-specific EFA index for gender and the survival rate to grade 5 for education quality.

这句话虽然有点长，但冒号后面是名词短语并列，所以逻辑关系不难分析。整句话拟译为：

全民教育发展指数中每个目标均有一个替代性指标：普及初等教育的净入学率、15岁及以上成人扫盲人群中的识字率、针对性别的全民教育指数以及教育质量中小学五年级的续读率。

（2）They are unlikely to achieve EFA by 2015 without dramatically stepped-up efforts, including international support, though there is very rapid and encouraging change among many of the countries with the lowest indicators.

这一句包含though引导的让步状语从句，但是由于前面主句的主语和后面从句的主语并不指同一批国家，所以最好不要将从句提前。可以考虑如下翻译：

这些国家如果不加紧努力（包括国际援助），很难于2015年前实现全民教育。当然，许多指数最低的国家也发生了迅速而可喜的变化。

参考译文

全民教育发展指数（EDI）于2003年开始引入，为各国的全民教育状况提供了总体衡量标准。该指数包括4个目标：普及初等教育、成人扫盲、男女教育平等以及教育质量。所使用的数据还不够标准，无法把儿童早期的培养和教育以及生活技能纳入其中。全民教育发展指数中每个目标均有一个替代性指标：普及初等教育的净入学率、15岁及以上成人扫盲人群中的识字率、针对性别的全民教育指数以及教育质量中小学五年级的续读率。全民教育发展指数在0－1之间，1代表已实现全民教育。2002年的指数基于123个国家的数据计算，因为从这些国家中能获得四个方面的数据。结果显示：

- 46个国家的全民教育发展指数大于0.95，因此可以视为这些国家已达到或接近于全民教育。这些国家大部分位于北美洲和欧洲，几十年来一直实施义务教育。
- 各个地区中49个国家的全民教育发展指数在0.80到0.94之间。教育质量仍然是拉丁美洲和加勒比地区的一个问题。阿拉伯国家中，较低的成人识字率降低了全民教育发展指数。
- 28个国家的全民教育发展指数低于0.80，其中有一多半分布在撒哈拉以南的非洲地区。这些国家中，全民教育发展指数的四个目标均保持较低的水平。这些国家如果不加紧努力（包括国际援助），很难于2015年前实现全民教育。当然，许多指数最低的国家也发生了迅速而可喜的变化。

第三模块：中文政府与组织文件语篇英译解析

原文

当前，全球互联网治理体系变革进入关键时期，构建网络空间命运共同体日益成为国际社会的广泛共识。互联网和信息技术迅猛发展，在为经济和社会发展注入强劲动力的同时，也给世界各国主权、安全、发展利益带来许多新的挑战。站在全球互联网治理体系变革的关键节点，没有哪个国家能够独自应对人类面临的各种挑战，也没有哪个国家能够退回到自我封闭的孤岛。网络空间是人类共同的活动空间，网络空间前途命运应由世界各国共同掌握。各国应该加强沟通、扩大共识、深化合作，共同构建网络空间命运共同体。只有各国共同发展，数字经济的发展红利才能在更大范围内充分释放和涌流；只有携手合作，才能有效地应对日益严峻的网络犯罪、网络恐怖主义等安全威胁和挑战。

网络空间命运共同体的内容在实践中不断丰富。命运共同体首先是安全共同体，各国既要携手应对网络犯罪、网络恐怖主义等共同的安全威胁，更要携手打造一个和平的网络空间，反对网络空间军备竞赛，坚持以和平方式解决网络空间的冲突和争端。命运共同体也是发展共同体，经济和社会发展是所有国家的共同愿景，要促进数字经济合作，推动网络空间相关资本、技术、信息、人才等要素的流动和共享，共同加强能力建设，互利互惠，实现共同发展。命运共同体还是文化共同体，要培育积极向上的共同价值观，促进各国优秀文化的交流互鉴，文明的多样性不应当成为冲突源泉，和而不同、兼容并蓄的文化交流才是世界和平发展的应有之义。

翻译解析

本篇节选自中国互联网发展报告，主题是网络空间命运共同体。里面既有一些关于网络的专业术语，也有中国提出的重要概念，更有一些长句，翻译时要特别注意。下面详细解析重点问题。

1. 专业术语

本篇出现的网络空间专业术语基本按照原文进行翻译即可，但要将英语放在网上核实一下，看是否是英语常用的表达。主要专业术语及其翻译如下：

（1）　全球互联网治理体系：global Internet governance system

（2）　网络空间：cyberspace

（3）　信息技术：information technology

（4）　网络犯罪：cybercrime

（5）　网络恐怖主义：cyberterrorism

2. 中国提出的重要概念

本篇出现了一些中国概念，既有新兴词汇，也有传统概念，翻译这些概念时先查证是否已有官方译文，已有的基本可以直接使用。如果没有官方翻译，可以自己根据意思翻译，译文应言简意赅。主要概念及其翻译如下：

（1）　网络空间命运共同体：a community of shared future in cyberspace

（2）　命运共同体：a community of shared future

（3）　发展共同体：a community of development

（4） 交流互鉴：exchanges and mutual learning

（5） 和而不同：harmoniously diversified

（6） 兼容并蓄：inclusive

“人类命运共同体”译为 a global community of shared future，所以这里的“共同体”均模仿此翻译，译为community。“和而不同”可以用英语的主从结构，即harmoniously diversified；“兼容并蓄”前后意思相似，所以只需译成一个单词inclusive。

3. 渲染词

本篇也有一些渲染语气的词，翻译时需要低调处理。主要有以下几处：

（1）成为国际社会的广泛共识

这里的“广泛”是渲染语气的词，与后面的“共识”在意义上有重复之处，整个短语可以译为become a consensus of the international community。

（2）有效地应对

这里的“有效”也可以视为渲染语气的词，最好不要译出，只翻译“应对”，译成cope with即可。

4. 重复名词

汉语语篇中，同一名词重复是常见现象，可以视为汉语语篇一种重要的衔接手段，但是英语中最好不要重复同一名词，而是使用替代作为语篇衔接的手段。下面一段话中“各国”使用了三次，为了保证英语语篇的衔接与连贯，建议可以将第一句和第二句合并，第一句后半部分可以译成被动语态，即be jointly controlled by all countries，那么第二句就能够使用非限定性定语从句放在后面。第三句中的“各国”则可以使用they替代。原文和译文如下：

网络空间是人类共同的活动空间，网络空间前途命运应由世界各国共同掌握。各国应该加强沟通、扩大共识、深化合作，共同构建网络空间命运共同体。只有各国共同发展，数字经济的发展红利才能在更大范围内充分释放和涌流。

Cyberspace is a common space for human activities, so it should be jointly controlled by all countries, who should strengthen communication, expand consensus, deepen cooperation, and build a community of shared future in cyberspace. Only when they develop together can the development dividend of the digital economy be fully released.

5. 长句

本篇有几个长句，每个句子由多个小分句组成。翻译这些句子时，要根据英语句子结构特点，使用一些主从结构，也可以拆译成多个句子。具体如下：

（1）互联网和信息技术迅猛发展，在为经济和社会发展注入强劲动力的同时，也给世界各国主权、安全、发展利益带来许多新的挑战。

这句话虽然比较长，但主干成分就是“发展注入动力，也带来挑战”，因此只需译成一个句子，其他修饰成分处理为定语。拟译如下：

The rapid development of the Internet and information technology has not only injected strong impetus into economic and social development, but also posed many new challenges for the sovereignty, security, and development of all countries.

（2）命运共同体首先是安全共同体，各国既要携手应对网络犯罪、网络恐怖主义等共同的安全威胁，更要携手打造一个和平的网络空间，反对网络空间军备竞赛，坚持以和平方式解决网络空间的冲突和争端。

经过分析可以看出，本句的第一个小分句“命运共同体首先是安全共同体”其实是整句的主题句，所以建议单独成句。后面的部分根据关联词“既要……”“更要……”可以拆分成两句话。这样，最后一句就变成了一个无主句，但根据上文可知主语是“各国”，所以可以用代词they表示。整句话拟译为：

First and foremost, a community of shared future is a community of security. Countries should work together to address common security threats such as cybercrime and terrorism. More importantly, they should work together to build peaceful cyberspace, oppose arms race in cyberspace, and resolve conflicts and disputes by peaceful means.

（3）命运共同体还是文化共同体，要培育积极向上的共同价值观，促进各国优秀文化的交流互鉴，文明的多样性不应当成为冲突源泉，和而不同、兼容并蓄的文化交流才是世界和平发展的应有之义。

这句话的分析和前面的句子相似，其中“命运共同体还是文化共同体”是主题句，所以单独翻译成一句话。第二部分“要培育积极向上的共同价值观，促进各国优秀文化的交流互鉴”在语义上可以和后面拆分开，成为一个无主句，翻译时需要添加主语we。最后的两个分句之间有转折之意，可以翻译成并列句，用while连接。整句话拟译为：

A community of shared future is a cultural community. We should foster positive common values and promote exchanges and mutual learning among fine cultures of all countries. Diversity of civilizations should not be a source of conflict, while harmoniously diversified and inclusive cultural exchange is beneficial to the world's peace and development.

参考译文

As the reform of the global Internet governance system is entering a critical period, building a community of shared future in cyberspace has increasingly become a consensus of the international community. The rapid development of the Internet and information technology has not only injected strong impetus into economic and social development, but also posed many new challenges for the sovereignty, security, and development of all countries. At a critical stage of the global Internet governance system change, no country can deal alone with the challenges faced by human beings and no country can retreat into an isolated island. Cyberspace is a common space for human activities, so it should be jointly controlled by all countries, who should strengthen communication, expand consensus, deepen cooperation, and build a community of shared future in cyberspace. Only when they develop together can the development dividend of the digital economy be fully released; only by working together can we cope with the increasingly serious security threats and challenges such as cybercrime and cyberterrorism.

The content of a community of shared future in cyberspace has been enriched in practice. First and foremost, a community of shared future is a community of security. Countries should work together to address common security threats such as cybercrime and terrorism. More importantly, they should work together to build peaceful cyberspace, oppose arms race in cyberspace, and resolve conflicts and disputes by peaceful means. A community of shared future is also a community of development. Economic and social development is the vision of all countries. We should promote cooperation in digital economy, facilitate the flow and sharing of capital, technology, information, talent and other factors related to cyberspace, work together to strengthen energy development, and achieve mutual benefit and development. A community of shared future is a cultural community. We should foster positive common values and promote exchanges and mutual learning among fine cultures of all countries. Diversity of civilizations should not be a source of conflict, while harmoniously diversified and inclusive cultural exchange is beneficial to the world's peace and development.

第四模块：翻译练习

1. 英译中

Based on the provisions of the CEDAW and the Beijing Platform for Action, progress has been achieved, in particular in the following areas:

Legal reform, aiming at the elimination of discrimination and the further safeguarding of women's rights in all fields of law and, in particular, in Family and Labour Law, has been pursued, bringing national laws in line with relevant international instruments.

Economic independence of women has been pursued through measures facilitating the reconciliation of working and family responsibilities, promoting equal pay and the protection of maternity, the improvement of vocational guidance and training, and schemes to support women's entrepreneurship.

Balanced representation of men and women in politics has been pursued through training programs aimed at encouraging and supporting women to enter politics and at creating a friendlier environment for women within political parties.

2. 中译英

国际网络空间治理应该坚持多边参与、多方参与，发挥政府、国际组织、互联网企业、技术社群、民间机构、公民个人等各种主体作用。既要推动联合国框架内的网络治理，也要更好地发挥各类非国家行为体的积极作用。

互联互通是网络空间的基本属性，也是保持互联网创新活力、持续发展的根本保证。加强网络空间开放合作，是构建网络空间命运共同体的重要目标。要在开放的基础上推动不同层次的双边、区域和国际合作，共同搭建沟通与合作的交流平台，强化资源优势互补，实现共同发展。

第十单元 新闻

第一模块：新闻翻译概述

新闻翻译指的是有关时事、社会热点等报道的翻译。中英文新闻报道一般具有简洁明晰、用词生动、表达准确客观等特点，强调内容的时效性、趣味性、简洁性及准确性等。新闻翻译要注重体现新闻的文体风格，同时又要注意目的语读者对新闻文体的期待，所以不能晦涩难懂，在用词和句式结构上要多加锤炼。中英文新闻文体在具体的风格表现方面既有差异，也有相同点，翻译时要多加注意。下面分别讨论中英文新闻的文体特点及其翻译。

一、英文新闻文体特点及其翻译

（一）用词特点

英语新闻中常用的表达，往往体现特定的新闻色彩。比如常用say、according to the eyewitness/source concerned等表示消息来源，常用with guarded reserve（谨慎态度）、no comments（无可奉告）、in response to allegation in *China Daily*（就《中国日报》的提法发表评论）等。这些词汇一般直接翻译即可。

英语新闻用语要考虑到广大的读者，所以用词相对简单。这类词汇翻译时也尽量简单。例如：

例1

Researchers have highlighted Asia, Europe, and North America as three potential hot spots for energy generation.

研究人员将亚洲、欧洲和北美洲定为三个潜在能源生产热点地区。

例2

British lawmaker Sir David Amess was stabbed to death in an Essex church on Friday by an assailant who lunged at him as he met voters, in what police said was a terrorist attack.

英国议员戴维·艾梅斯爵士星期五在埃塞克斯郡一教堂会见选民时遭到一名男子刺杀身亡，警方称此事件为恐怖袭击。

英语新闻中常用缩略语，以节省时间和篇幅。缩略语翻译时需要译出全称，这样中文读者才能明白。例如AP（Associated Press，美联社）、HSI（Hang Seng Index，恒生指数）。特别是新闻标题中的缩略语使用就更加频繁。请看下面的例子：

例3

UN Security Council Extends Mandate of Political Mission in Haiti

联合国安理会延长驻海地政治特派团任期

新闻正文中的缩略语有时候会在后面的括号内给出全称，也有时候先写全称，再写缩略语。这两种情况下，翻译就简单多了，直接译出全称即可。例如：

例4

The water delivered includes more than one million liters of drinking water and 1.7 million liters of water for sanitation, said the UN Office for the Coordination of Humanitarian Affairs (OCHA).

联合国人道主义事务协调办公室表示，输送的水包括100多万升饮用水和170万升卫生用水。

例5

The police said that they received information about the incident on October 11, adding that the MLC (Medico-Legal Case) was also done.

警方称已于10月11日收到有关事件的信息，还称已经进行了法医鉴定。

英语新闻为体现时效性，经常根据社会发展使用新词，例如Euromart（欧洲共同市场）、supercrat（高级官员）、sitcom（情景喜剧）、masscult（大众文化）、mortgage slave（房奴）等。

（二）句式特点

英语新闻中首先常使用简单句，特别是扩展的简单句。由于新闻报道一般出现在报纸上，需优先篇幅，因此会将更多信息压缩在简单句中，常使用一些短语做定语或者状语。翻译时也尽量使用简短的汉语句子。例如：

例6

Officials in the US and several other countries have now authorized booster shots for various subsets of their populations.

美国和其他几个国家的官员已授权为一些人群注射加强针。

例7

In 2016, a week before the country's divisive Brexit referendum, Cox, a Labour Party lawmaker, was fatally stabbed and shot in northern England.

2016年，在英国脱欧公投倒数一星期之际，工党议员考克斯在英格兰北部遭刀袭和枪击身亡。

当然，英语新闻中还有一些带有定语从句或宾语从句的句子，定语从句一般较短，宾语从句一般用于援引某人的话或观点。

例8

Yet some people, especially those who are immunocompromised, may not mount a strong response to the initial doses.

但有些人群，特别是免疫缺失人群，可能不会对第一剂疫苗产生较强的反应。

例9

Texas is now poised to join seven other states that passed similar laws this year, part of a national campaign in which Republican legislators introduced such bills in 32 states.

得克萨斯州准备加入今年通过类似法律的其他七个州，这是一项全国运动的组成部分，该运动中，共和党议员在32个州引入了该类法案。

例10

Conservatives say the law, which applies to public school teams through high school, is protecting fair competition.

保守党称该法适用于公立学校高中团体，可保护公平竞争。

例11

Conservative Prime Minister said he and his Cabinet were "deeply shocked and heart-stricken."

保守党首相曾表示自己和内阁感到"非常震惊和痛心"。

从上述例子可以看出，定语从句的翻译要看定语从句的长短，是限定性还是非限定性从句，从而决定是前置还是后置。宾语从句则可以直接翻译。

正是由于定语从句和宾语从句使用较多，新闻英语中有些句子显得长而复杂。翻译长句之前需要厘清其中的逻辑关系，本书已经多次讲过长句的翻译，所以这里不再赘述。例如：

例12

Tokyo was facing the prospect of its first blackouts in nearly two decades yesterday after the city's main power company shut down the last of its 17 nuclear reactors for safety checks, after a series of damaging scandals.

一系列破坏性丑闻爆出后，东京的主要电力公司昨天关闭了17个核反应堆中的最后一个，以便进行安全检查。此事令东京市民近20年来第一次陷入了无电可用的境况。

例13

Just advanced by the Russians and later picked up and made much of by certain American writers, was the claim that U-2 pilots were worried that if the device had to be used, the CIA had rigged it in such a way that it would be exploded prematurely, thus eliminating, in one great blast, all incriminating evidence, the plane, and pilots.

U-2飞行员担心，中央情报局已在飞机上安放了一种装置，该装置如有需要会提前爆炸，把飞机、驾驶员和全部证据一下子化为乌有。这种说法最先由俄罗斯人提出，后被美国一些作家大肆宣传。

英语新闻中常用被动语态，来强调动作的承受者，或无需说出动作的发出者，抑或是保护消息来源等等。请看下面的例子：

十

例14

Amess, 69, *was attacked* around midday Friday at a Methodist church in Leigh-on-Sea, a town about 40 miles (about 64 kilometers) east of London.

现年69岁的艾梅斯周五中午在滨海利的卫理公会教堂遇袭。滨海利距离伦敦东部约40英里（约64公里）。

例15

While information labeled confidential could be declassified automatically in as soon as 10 years, mid-level secret information would be kept classified for at least 20 years and top secret information for a minimum of 30 years, but extensions could be made for up to 90 years.

定位秘密级的情报最快可在10年内自动解密，中等密级的情报则至少需保留20年，绝密情报至少需保留30年，部分情报的解密期可长达90年。

例16

The extradition case was political, the court was told.

有人在法庭上陈述说，这起引渡案是政治性的。

例14原文旨在强调动作的承受者，而且被动语态中的动词对于主语来说是不愿意发生的。这类被动语态可以直接译成中文被动语态，当然不一定要使用“被”字，可以使用其同义词，如“受”“遭”“挨”“（遭）遇”等，这里翻译成“遇袭”，就表达了被动意义。除此之外，英语被动语态大多要译成主动语态。例15原文使用被动语态是因为没有必要说出动作的发出者，例16是为了保护消息来源（即动作的发出者），这两个例子均转译为汉语的主动语态。

（三）标题特点

新闻标题是新闻的重要组成部分，更是新闻内容的高度概括和凝练，旨在吸引读者的眼球，同时也帮助读者选择自己想看的新闻。英语新闻标题往往简明扼要，一般会使用短语或非完整句，省略一定的冠词、助动词等，即使有的使用句子，句子也尽量简短，同时使用一般现在时体现新闻的时效性。比如，“Streets Deserted as Strikes Begin”“Disney Rail Link to Create 1,000 Jobs”等。

有鉴于此，英语新闻标题的翻译既要准确传达原文的意思，又要做到言简意赅，富有文采和创意，这样才能保证吸引中文的读者。请看下面的例子：

例17

Food Drops "Great TV" but Almost Useless

空投食品无异作秀 杯水车薪于事无补

例18

Cargo Park for Airport "to Deliver 2,000 Jobs"

机场拟建大型货场 就业职位至少两千

以上两个例子原文符合英语新闻标题的特点，中文翻译也尽量简洁，可以使用一些四字格，使得译文更富有魅力和表现力，从而用标题先吸引住读者。

二、中文新闻文体特点及其翻译

（一）用词特点

中文新闻中会经常使用“据悉……”“据报道……”“根据……调查”“根据……预计”“统计数据显示……”“另有消息称……”“从……处了解到……”“……指出……”等提示语，这些提示语可以用say、according to、it is learned等来翻译。例如：

例19

据报道，在公安部和河北省警方的共同努力下，三名犯罪嫌疑人于周一在湖北襄阳被抓获。

It said that the three suspects were captured in Xiangyang, Hubei Province, on Monday through the combined efforts of the Ministry of Public Security and police in Hebei Province.

例20

统计数据显示，截至2022年底，超过14%的中国人（约2.67亿人）年龄在60岁以上。

Statistics show that by the end of 2022, more than 14 percent of the Chinese people (or about 267 million people) were aged above 60.

中文新闻中还经常使用一些简称（即中文缩略语），这些简称大多可以根据意思进行翻译。例如，“入遗”译成 to be listed into the World Cultural

Heritages，“简政放权”可以译成to streamline government administration and delegate power，“三农问题”译成issues of agriculture, rural areas, and rural people。但是，当缩略语在新闻中第一次出现时，可以先简单翻译，括号内进行解释，下文再出现时便可以直接使用简单翻译。请看下面的例子：

例21

“五位一体”总体布局

Five-Sphere Integrated Plan (to promote coordinated economic, political, cultural, social, and ecological advancement)

例22

两会

Two Sessions (the National People's Congress and the Chinese People's Political Consultative Conference)

例23

“两弹一星”计划

Two Bombs and One Satellite project (Two Bombs refer to the nuclear bombs and the missile, while One Satellite refers to the space satellite)

随着时代的发展，中文新闻中还会使用一些新词，以吸引读者的眼球。这些新词可以根据意思进行翻译，有些新词如果无法简单地译出，则可使用音译，括号内再补充解释。请看下面的一些例子：

（1） 代驾：designated driver

（2） 跳槽：job-hop

（3） 退居二线：retire from the leading post

（4） 直播带货：live-streaming marketing/commerce

（5） 点赞：give a like

（6） 自拍：selfie

（7） 裸婚：*luohun* (getting married without a house, a car, a wedding ring or even a wedding ceremony)

（8） 灌水：*guanshui* (publish meaningless comments on the web)

（二）句式特点

中文新闻经常使用无主句，无主句不用说出动作的发出者，可以显现新闻所提供信息的客观性。在翻译这些无主句时，要根据所表达的语气添加主语或者变成被动语态。请看下面的例子：

例24

下一阶段，将聚焦群众“急难愁盼”问题，在推动有条件的楼宇加装电梯、完善老旧小区物业管理等方面加大力度，不断增强人民群众的获得感、幸福感、安全感。

For the next stage, the focus will be put on what people find urgent and difficult and what they are worried and anxious about. We will promote the installation of elevators in buildings with necessary conditions and improve the property management of old neighborhoods to enhance the people's sense of gain, happiness, and security.

例25

对新型室内娱乐场所，要加强管理，监督检查严格落实各项疫情防控措施。

Management and supervision over the pandemic prevention and control measures will be enhanced for new types of indoor places of amusement.

例26

加强智慧法院建设，扎实推进信息技术与知识产权审判融合促进。

Smart courts will be built to promote the integration and mutual contribution between information technology and intellectual property trials.

中文新闻的句子一般动词短语连用比较多，句式较长，但大多都是并列小分句。翻译这类长句时，要厘清各部分的关系，找到主结构，其他结构需判断是做定语还是状语，如果是状语要看是表目的还是结果等等。请看下面的例子：

例27

数据成果全面客观反映了我国国土利用状况，也反映出耕地保护、生态建设、节约集约用地方面存在的问题，必须采取有针对性的措施加以改进。

对例27进行分析可以看出，主结构是“数据成果全面客观反映了……也反映出……”，这里虽然重复使用“反映”一词，但翻译时可以使用一个谓语动词。这一部分和后面的“必须采取有针对性的措施加以改进”可视为因果关系，因此后面可以用连词so引出。整个译文如下：

The data comprehensively and objectively reflect the status of China's land use, and problems in the protection of arable land, ecological construction, optimal and intensive land use, so targeted measures must be taken for improvement.

例28

要根据我国经济发展状况，充分考虑世界科学技术加快发展和国际经济结构加速重组的趋势，着眼于全面提高国民经济整体素质和效益，增强综合国力和国际竞争力，对经济结构进行战略性调整。

对例28进行分析会发现，这句话的语义重心是“对经济结构进行战略性调整”，其目的是“全面提高国民经济整体素质和效益，增强综合国力和国际竞争力”，最前面的部分是背景和前提。这样分析后即可确定在译文中将背景和前提放在主结构的前面，目的放在主结构的后面。整句话翻译如下：

In line with China's economic development, the world's accelerated progress in science and technology, and the speedy restructuring of the international economy, we should strategically restructure our economy to improve the quality and performance of the entire national economy in an all-round way and the overall national strength and international competitiveness.

（三）标题特点

中文新闻标题和英语新闻标题一样，一般言简意赅，形象生动，旨在追求生动醒目。请看下面的例子：

例29

质量不合格眼药水下架

Poor-quality Eye Drops off Shelves

例30

三军仪仗队首次设立女兵方阵

First Chinese Female Honor Guards Joining the Parade

例31

迪士尼紧急停止游客进入

Entry into Disneyland Temporarily Suspended

以上三个例子的原文标题均比较简单，翻译时尽量简短，均使用短语。如果使用句子，尽量用一般现在时，体现时效性。

三、新闻翻译原则与策略归纳

综上所述，新闻翻译也需要遵循特定的原则：(1) 新闻翻译需要准确传达信息，因为新闻文本属于信息文体，以传达信息为主，体现新闻的真实性。(2) 新闻翻译要注意用词准确，特别是英语缩写和中文简称的翻译要准确，从而保证不会给目的语读者造成误解或者阅读障碍。(3) 新闻翻译要注意中英文句式结构和语态，准确地传达原文的视角和立场。(4) 新闻标题翻译要言简意赅。总之，新闻翻译要注意尽量获得译文受众的认同。新闻的文体特点和翻译策略可归纳为下表：

英译中

	英文新闻文体特点	翻译策略
词汇	用词相对简单	译成相对简单的中文词汇
	缩略语使用较多	译出全称
句式	简单句	汉语也尽量简单
	名词性从句	根据行文习惯进行调整
	长句	分析逻辑关系，根据中文表达习惯进行调整。
标题	简洁，高度凝练。	尽量简洁，但要吸引中文读者。

中译英

	中文新闻文体特点	翻译策略
词汇	表示消息来源的提示语	可以使用according to、it is learned 等表达。
	简称（缩略表达）	大多可以意译，有些可以先直译，然后在括号内进行解释。
	新词	大多可以意译，有个别意译过于复杂时，可以先采用直译或音译，然后在括号内进行解释。
句式	无主句	根据原文的语气添加主语或者转译为被动语态。
	长句（动词短语并列使用频繁）	厘清动词短语之间的逻辑关系，找到主结构，然后根据分析出来的逻辑关系将其他动词短语译为定语或状语。
标题	言简意赅	尽量简洁

第二模块：英文新闻语篇汉译解析

原文

十

Even as schools have returned in full swing across America, complications wrought by the pandemic persist, often falling hardest on those least able to weather them: families without transportation, people with limited income or other financial hardship, people who don't speak English, and children with special needs.

Coronavirus outbreaks in school and individual quarantine orders when students get exposed to the virus make it a gamble on whether they can attend classes in person on any given day. Many families don't know where to turn for information, or sometimes can't be reached.

And sometimes, because of driver shortages, it's as simple as the school bus not showing up.

Keiona Morris, who lives without a car in McKeesport, Pennsylvania, outside Pittsburgh, has had no choice but to keep her boys at home on days when the bus didn't arrive. Her two sons have missed about two weeks' worth of classes because of such disruptions, she said.

Taking her older son to school on the civic bus system those days would mean not making it home in time to get her youngest to elementary school, she said.

"I feel like they're leaving my kid behind," Morris said. "Sometimes, he feels like he's not important enough to get picked up."

For some families, it's a matter of not having the private resources to deal with breakdowns in the public education system. For others, language barriers or other communication issues leave them uninformed about things like programs that let students return to school despite virus exposures, as long as they test negative for infection.

翻译解析

本篇是关于新冠疫情对美国学校影响的报道，时效性很强。里面有一些新闻用语，如援引某人的话，还有一些关于新冠疫情的词汇。句式结构有短有长，特别是一些长句需要注意。下面详细分析。

1. 关于新冠疫情词汇

（1） pandemic：流行病，疫情

（2） coronavirus：冠状病毒

（3） quarantine：隔离

（4） negative：阴性的

（5） infection：感染

2. 援引别人的提示语

由于是新闻报道，本篇有三个地方援引了别人的话，其中两处是she said，还有一处是Morris said。这里的said可以直接译成“说”，也可以译成“表示”。

3. 长句

本篇有几个句子比较长，翻译时需要注意先理解其中的逻辑关系，然后再进行翻译。

（1）Even as schools have returned in full swing across America, complications wrought by the pandemic persist, often falling hardest on those least able to weather them: families without transportation, people with limited income or other financial hardship, people who don't speak English, and children with special needs.

这句话冒号前面的主结构是complications wrought by the pandemic persist，该部分前后都有状语，这样对主从结构进行分析后发现可以按照原文的顺序进行翻译。冒号后面是对those的解释，每个中心词后面均跟了定语，有的是短语，有的是从句，但不难理解，译文可以考虑将定语前置。整句话拟译如下：

尽管美国各地的学生都纷纷返校，疫情带来的负面影响仍在持续。其中最易遭受冲击、困难最大的群体包括：没有交通出行工具的家庭，收入有限或其他经济困难的人群，不懂英语的群体以及有特殊需求的儿童。

（2）Coronavirus outbreaks in school and individual quarantine orders when students get exposed to the virus make it a gamble on whether they can attend classes in person on any given day.

这句话的主结构是Coronavirus outbreaks in school and individual quarantine orders ... make it a gamble。前面的并列主语都是名词结构，呈静态，建议翻译成汉语的小分句，整句话拟译为：

冠状病毒可能在校园蔓延，学生接触病毒后需单独隔离，这导致学生每天能否到校上课成为未知数。

（3）Keiona Morris, who lives without a car in McKeesport, Pennsylvania, outside Pittsburgh, has had no choice but to keep her boys at home on days when the bus didn't arrive.

这句话的主语Keiona Morris后面紧跟一个非限定性定语从句，该从句没有译为前置定语，而是译为谓语成分，与句子主语构成一个小分句。需要注意的是，该定语从句中的without a car解释了下文的原因，因此可将其单独拿出来，作为原因状语承接下文。拟译如下：

基奥娜·莫里斯住在宾夕法尼亚州匹兹堡郊外的麦基斯波特，由于自己没有车，校车不来的时候，只能让两个儿子待在家里。

（4）For others, language barriers or other communication issues leave them uninformed about things like programs that let students return to school despite virus exposures, as long as they test negative for infection.

这句话中，programs后面跟了that引导的定语从句，可以考虑先将前面翻译出来，定语从句处理为独立的句子而且后置。另外，句首的代词others根据前文可以判断是other families。整句话拟译为：

对于其他家庭而言，语言障碍或其他沟通问题使他们对一些机制一无所知。即使学生暴露在有病毒的环境中，只要检测结果呈阴性，这些机制也会允许学生到校上课。

4. 被动语态

本篇中出现的被动语态均需要转译成主动语态，其中两处分析如下。

（1）Many families don't know where to turn for information, or sometimes can't be reached.

句尾处的被动语态can't be reached是为了和前文主语保持一致，如果直译为被动语态会比较生硬，因此建议转译为主动语态。拟译为：

许多家庭不知道去哪里查询相关信息，有时则是学校无法与他们取得联络。

（2）Sometimes, he feels like he's not important enough to get picked up.

这里的get picked up实际上也是被动语态，在翻译时显然不能直译，需要转换成通顺的中文表达。拟译为：

有时候，孩子觉得自己不够重要，所以才没有车坐。

参考译文

尽管美国各地的学生都纷纷返校，疫情带来的负面影响仍在持续。其中最易遭受冲击、困难最大的群体包括：没有交通出行工具的家庭，收入有限或其他经济困难的人群，不懂英语的群体以及有特殊需求的儿童。

冠状病毒可能在校园蔓延，学生接触病毒后需单独隔离，这导致学生每天能否到校上课成为未知数。许多家庭不知道去哪里查询相关信息，有时则是学校无法与他们取得联络。

有时，由于司机人数不足，连校车都无法保证。

基奥娜·莫里斯住在宾夕法尼亚州匹兹堡郊外的麦基斯波特，由于自己没有车，校车不来的时候，只能让两个儿子待在家里。基奥娜说，由于这种影响，孩子们已经错过了约两周的课程。

基奥娜表示，这期间如果坐公交车送大儿子上学，就意味着不能及时赶回家送小儿子去学校。

"我觉得他们在抛弃我的孩子。"基奥娜说，"有时候，孩子觉得自己不够重要，所以才没有车坐。"

对一些家庭而言，问题在于没有私人资源来应对公共教育系统的崩溃。对于其他家庭而言，语言障碍或其他沟通问题使他们对一些机制一无所知。即使学生暴露在有病毒的环境中，只要检测结果呈阴性，这些机制也会允许学生到校上课。

第三模块：中文新闻语篇英译解析

原文

神舟十三号首次出舱活动圆满成功

据中国载人航天工程办公室消息，航天员翟志刚和王亚平圆满完成出舱活动全部既定任务，安全返回天和核心舱。

这是中国载人航天工程空间站阶段第三次航天员出舱活动，是神舟十三号航天员乘组首次出舱活动，也是中国航天史上首次有女航天员参加的出舱活动。

北京时间11月8日1时16分，经过6.5小时的出舱活动，航天员乘组返回核心舱。此次出舱活动进一步检验了我国新一代舱外航天服的功能性能，检验了航天员与机械臂协同工作的能力及出舱活动相关支持设备的可靠性与安全性。神舟十三号载人飞船于10月16日成功发射，顺利将三名航天员送入太空，他们将在轨驻留六个月。

航天员出舱活动期间，天地间大力协同、舱内外密切配合，先后完成了机械臂悬挂装置与转接件安装、舱外典型动作测试等任务，全过程顺利圆满。

翻译解析

本篇报道的是我国神舟十三号出舱活动，属于时事新闻。里面有一些关于报道的提示语和航空航天的专业术语，个别句子较长。这些内容在翻译中均需要注意。下面详细分析。

1. 标题

按照本单元的讲解，新闻标题翻译要言简意赅，因此，本篇标题“神舟十三号首次出舱活动圆满成功”可以译成*Shenzhou XIII* Taikonauts Complete 1st Spacewalk，标题使用一般现在时，突出时效性。

2. 专有名词和专业术语

本篇出现了“神舟十三号”等专有名词以及一些航天领域的术语，翻译时要表达准确。具体罗列如下：

（1） 神舟十三号：*Shenzhou XIII*

（2） 中国载人航天工程办公室：China Manned Space Agency (CMSA)

（3） 中国航天员：taikonaut（该词是由中文“太空”的拼音和英语单词astronaut混成的拼缀词，已被词典收录，意思为“中国宇航员”）

（4） 出舱活动：extravehicular activities (EVAs)

（5） 核心舱：core module

（6） 舱外航天服：extravehicular spacesuit

（7） 机械臂：mechanical arm

（8） 支持设备：supporting equipment

（9） 舱外典型动作：extravehicular maneuver

3. 报道提示语

本篇第一段开头“据中国载人航天工程办公室消息”属于报道提示语，可以译为the China Manned Space Agency (CMSA) said，这一部分可以按照英语的表达习惯放在所说内容的后面。当然，也可以放在句首译成 According to the China Manned Space Agency (CMSA)。

4. 长句

本篇有两个句子比较长，翻译时注意分析，找到主次结构即可。

（1）此次出舱活动进一步检验了我国新一代舱外航天服的功能性能，检验了航天员与机械臂协同工作的能力及出舱活动相关支持设备的可靠性与安全性。

这句话的主谓结构实际上就是“此次出舱活动进一步检验了……”，其中“检验”后面有三个宾语，即“我国新一代舱外航天服的功能性能”“航天员与机械臂协同工作的能力”和“出舱活动相关支持设备的可靠性与安全性”。分析之后，翻译就简单了。拟译如下：

The mission further tested the functions of the China-developed new-generation extravehicular spacesuits, the coordination between the taikonauts and the mechanical arm, and the reliability and safety of supporting equipment related to the EVAs.

（2）航天员出舱活动期间，天地间大力协同、舱内外密切配合，先后完成了机械臂悬挂装置与转接件安装、舱外典型动作测试等任务，全过程顺利圆满。

这句话第一个逗号前是时间状语，“天地间大力协同、舱内外密切配合”是原因，后面的部分是无主句，可以考虑使用被动语态。整句话拟译为：

During the EVAs, thanks to the coordination between the three taikonauts and ground staff, and between the two outside the spaceship and the one inside, new components on the station's robotic arm were mounted and extravehicular maneuvers were practiced successfully.

参考译文

Shenzhou XIII Taikonauts Complete 1st Spacewalk

Taikonauts Zhai Zhigang and Wang Yaping have completed their extravehicular activities (EVAs) and returned to the space station core module *Tianhe*, the China Manned Space Agency (CMSA) said.

The event was the third extravehicular mission conducted during the construction of the country's space station and the first by the *Shenzhou XIII* crew. It also marks the first EVAs in Chinese space history involving a female taikonaut.

The pair returned to the core module at 1:16 am on Nov. 8 (Beijing time) after 6.5 hours of extravehicular activities. The mission further tested the functions of the China-developed new-generation extravehicular spacesuits, the coordination between the taikonauts and the mechanical arm, and the reliability and safety of supporting equipment related to the EVAs. China launched the *Shenzhou XIII* spaceship on Oct. 16, sending three taikonauts on a six-month mission to construct its space station.

During the EVAs, thanks to the coordination between the three taikonauts and ground staff, and between the two outside the spaceship and the one inside, new components on the station's robotic arm were mounted and extravehicular maneuvers were practiced successfully.

第四模块：翻译练习

十

1. 英译中

An earthquake of magnitude 4.8 struck Indonesia's Bali island on Saturday morning, killing at least three people, Indonesia's search and rescue agency said.

The quake affected the Karangasem and Bangli districts on the eastern side of the tourist island and a search has been concluded, the agency said in a statement, but authorities were continuing to monitor situation.

A landslide triggered by the quake killed two of the victims, the agency said. A third was killed by falling debris.

The United States Geological Survey (USGS) said the 4.8 magnitude quake struck off Banjar Wangsian, and put its depth at 10 km (about 6.21 miles).

There was no significant damage in other parts of Bali, while the quake was felt also in the neighboring island of Lombok, local media reported.

Bali reopened for international tourists on Thursday after 18 months of pandemic restrictions, but they are only expected to start arriving later this month.

2. 中译英

10月18日至26日，大型京剧交响套曲《京城大运河》在上海、杭州、南京、扬州、南通、宁波和苏州七个城市进行巡演。这部“北京大戏”由北京市文化和旅游局出品，北京文化艺术基金资助，北京交响乐团、北京京剧院、北京音协合唱团联手打造。

《京城大运河》是我国第一部以京城大运河为题材的舞台艺术作品，以传统京剧与西方交响乐融合的形式，描摹大运河北京段历史发展脉络，彰显北京城独树一帜的历史文化风貌。这部作品包括序曲和《一支塔影见通州》《天上的星星郭守敬》《漂来的北京城》《致敬大运河》四个乐章，综合舞美、灯光、服装、多媒体等多种舞台元素呈现，阵容庞大，气势恢宏。

附录一　常用公示语

Admission by Ticket Only 凭票入场
Admission Free 免费入场
Airport Lounge 机场休息室
Airport Shuttle 机场摆渡
Approaching End of Expressway 即将驶出高速
Arrivals 进港
Avoid the Jams 避免交通堵塞
Baggage Claim 行李提取
Baggage Deposit 行李寄存
Beware of Pickpocket 谨防扒手
Bicycle Parking 自行车存放处
Bus Lane/Buses Only 公交路线专用车道
Bus Stop 公交站点
Business Hours 营业时间
Cars parked here without permission will be clamped. 未经允许在此停车将被扣押。
Certain stations are closed on public holidays. 假日某些车站关闭。
Check-in (Area) 办理登机区
Children and Women First 儿童、妇女优先
Coach 长途汽车
Complaint Box 意见箱
Construction Ahead, Detour 施工请绕行
Courtesy/Priority Seat 老弱病残孕专座
Crossroads/Intersection 交叉路口
Customers Lounge 旅客休息室
Dangerous Bend 弯道危险
Departure Station 出发站
Departure Times on Reverse 返航时间
Destination 终点站
Dogs Not Allowed 禁止携犬入内
Domestic Flights 国内航班
Double-decker Bus 双层公共汽车
Drive with Caution 小心驾驶
Emergency Exit 紧急出口

Entry to Expressway 高速入口
Exit to All Routes 各通道出口
Fasten Seat Belt 请系好安全带
Flight Connections 转机处
For Use Only in Case of Fire 灭火专用
Give Way 快车先行
Guest's Car Park 来客停车场
Help us to keep the tube litter free. 请协助我们保持地铁清洁卫生。
Information/Inquiry 问讯处
Insert Here 此处插入
Introductions 说明
Keep Away from Fire 切勿近火
Keep Clear of Entrance 请不要堵住入口
Keep Dry 保持干燥
Keep Hands Off 请勿手扶
Keep Left/Right 靠左/右
Keep Quiet 保持安静
Keep Top Side Up 请勿倒置
Keep your belongings with you at all times. 请随身携带你的行李。
Left Junction 左交叉口
Limited Parking 停车位有限
Look Left/Right 向左/右看
Lost and Found 失物招领
Low Bridge Ahead 前方桥低
Luggage from Flights 到港行李
Luggage must not be put in the gateway. 行李不准放在过道上。
Mechanical Help 车辆修理
Mind the Gap 注意站台缝隙
Mind/Watch Your Step 注意脚下
Missing People Help Line 走失求救热线
New Hours of Parking Control 停车控制新时段
No Angling 禁止垂钓
No Cycling in the School 校内禁止骑车
No Entry 禁止入内
No Honking 禁止鸣笛
No Litter 勿乱扔杂物
No Overtaking 禁止超车

No parking. Constantly in use. 此处经常使用，禁止停车。
No parking except for loading. 除装货外，禁止停车。
No parking in front of this gate. 门前禁止停车。
No parking, in use 24 hours a day. 此处24小时使用，禁止停车。
No parking or materials in front of doors. 门前不准停车或堆放杂物。
No Passing 禁止通行
No Photography 请勿拍照
No smoking except in designated area. 除指定区域外，禁止吸烟。
No Stopping (at Any Time) 禁止停车
No Thoroughfare 禁止穿行
No Through Road 此路不通
No Touching 请勿触摸
No trade or business vehicle unless authorized. 未经允许货车禁止通行。
No U-Turn 禁止掉头
No Visitors 游客止步
Not for Sale 恕不出售
Not valid on certain trains. 车票对某些列车无效。
Nothing/Something to Declare 无/有报关
Office Hours 办公时间
On Sale 削价出售
One-way Street 单行道
Open Here 此处开启
Parking for Taxis Only 只准许出租停
Parking Permitted 允许停车
Passport Control 入境检验
Peak Hours Only 只限高峰时段
Pedestrian Crossing Ahead 注意前方人行横道
Petrol Station 加油站
Please do not park in front of the barrier. 请不要在护栏前停车。
Please do not park. Garage in use. 车库使用，门前请不要停车。
Please Hold Handrail 抓好扶手
Please keep gateways clear. 请保持过道畅通。
Please retain your ticket for inspection. 请保留车票待检。
Post No Bills 请勿张贴
Protect Public Property 爱护公共财物
Queue Here 请在此排队
Reclaim Belt 取行李传送带

Reserved Seating 预订的座位
Return Fares 往返票价
Road Closed 此路封闭
Safety First 安全第一
Save Energy 节约能源
School Ahead, Slow Down 前方学校，减速慢行
Shooting Prohibited 禁止打猎
Short Stay 短暂停留
Single or Return Tickets 单程或往返票
Slow Down 减速行驶
Speed Limit of 48km/h 限速每小时48公里
Split Here 此处撕开
Staff Only 闲人免进/员工专用
Take Care Not to Leave Things Behind 当心不要丢失东西
Take Your Assigned Seat 对号入座
Temporarily Closed 暂停开放
Terminal Station 目的地车站
The last train this evening will be the service to ... 今晚最后一列火车是到……
The light indicates the door is not secured. 指示灯亮显示门未关好。
This coach is for holders of full fare. 本长途汽车专为持全程票者乘坐。
This is a pay and display car park. 此停车场自动交费并显示票据。
This Side Up 此面向上
This vehicle stops frequently. 随时停车。
Ticket Office 售票处
Ticket valid until ... 车票有效期到……
To ensure punctuality, this barrier may be closed up to one minute prior to departure of each train. 为确保准时发车，此门在发车前一分钟关闭。
Toilet Engaged/Occupied 厕所有人
Toll Free 免费通行
Tube to ... 地铁开往……
U-Turn 允许调头
VIP Car Park 贵宾停车场
Visitors Please Register 来宾登记
Welcome Aboard 欢迎登机
Wet Paint 油漆未干
When the bus is moving, do not distract the driver. 汽车行驶中，严禁与司机交谈。
Wipe your shoes and boots. 请擦去鞋上的泥土。

With permission, but at owner's risk. 允许存放，但后果自负。

You will be required to leave a deposit when you pick up the car. 取车时需交押金。

附录二　翻译练习参考答案

第一单元

1. 英译中

全球疫苗免疫联盟（Gavi）的影响力离不开其核心合作伙伴的支持，如世界卫生组织、联合国儿童基金会以及世界银行。全球疫苗免疫联盟在加强初级卫生保健方面发挥了关键作用，有利于进一步实现可持续发展目标之全民健康覆盖，确保不落下任何一个人。

全球疫苗免疫联盟还与捐助方开展合作，包括主权政府、私营部门基金会、企业、非政府组织、游说团体、专业和社区协会、学术界、疫苗生产商（含新兴市场疫苗生产商）、研究和技术卫生机构以及执行国政府等。

全球疫苗免疫联盟帮助数百万处于最弱势地位的儿童获取未充分利用的新疫苗，不断改变着人们的生活，有利于推动低收入国家经济发展，建设更加安全的世界。

2. 中译英

Shanghai Disneyland provides a magic, adventurous, and exciting experience for visitors of all ages. Let's have fun in Enchanted Storybook Castle, the largest castle in the Disney world, and explore the seven amazing parks: Mickey Avenue, Gardens of Imagination, Fantasyland, Adventure Isle, Treasure Cove, Tomorrowland, and Disney-Pixar Toy Story Land.

The first Disneyland in the world was established 60 years ago with the aim to bring back pure, innocent and merry memories, and offer its guests unforgettable experience. This spirit is carried on to today in Shanghai Disney Resort with brand new theme parks and special amusement facilities.

第二单元

1. 英译中

每次使用后请清洁剃须刀，以获得最佳效果。使用热水要当心，切记先检查水温是否太高，以防烫手。请勿使用毛巾或纸巾擦拭剃须刀头部件，否则可能会损坏刀头。

冲洗剃须刀头部件时，水可能会从剃须刀底座中滴出，这属于正常现象。建议将产品及其配件晾干后，再将保护盖罩在配件上或将剃须刀放入收纳袋中。请将保护盖盖在剃须刀上，以防积聚灰尘。

随附的附件可能因产品而异。包装盒上会显示随附于您产品的附件。

2. 中译英

- AR series routers can be installed in a 19-inch standard cabinet/rack. Cabinet/Rack purchased from other vendors must have enough space for equipment installation.
- If the distance between front and rear mounting rails is not within the required range, install guide rails or a tray in the cabinet/rack to support the chassis. Guide rails or trays are not delivered with the product and must be purchased separately.
- Cabinet/Rack mounting is not recommended for Wi-Fi capable routers.
- Power cables must be more than 10 cm away from signal cables.
- Optical fibers must be used with optical modules.
- The bend radius of optical fibers must be larger than 40 mm.
- For the ground cable, attach the M4 lug to the router and the M6 lug to the ground point.
- If your router uses AC power supply, use AC power cables in compliance with local standards.

第三单元

1. 英译中

该品牌倾情推出全新女士腕表系列：Diamantissima系列。该系列的五款腕表尺寸各异，以典雅、低调的细节展现女性魅力。每款腕表都有标志性的钻石纹，其灵感源自该品牌著名的帆布面料印花——独特的交叉装饰图案。该系列腕表以精致的表壳和极简抽象风格的表盘完美呈现了这一设计：表壳上蚀刻着钻石纹，表盘的整个装饰图案呈现出面料印花的效果。拥有低调魅力的Diamantissima系列为时尚女性提供了全新的精美腕表。

2. 中译英

As a well-known Chinese watch brand, it inherits the mightiness and nobility implied in its “crown” logo. By virtue of meticulous craftsmanship and aesthetic ingenuity, it has designed plenty of bestsellers leading the fashion and receiving compliments. Annual sales of over two million watches make it significant in Chinese watchmaking industry.

From initiating the brand-new advertisement before CCTV's daily news program in 1990s to a trend of hiring spokespeople; from the first try in micro-film marketing to new marketing strategy of national star tour, it has been leading the way for many years, promoting the development and changes in the industry.

第四单元

1. 英译中

即使与投资人青睐的战略不一致，公司也应该履行自己的承诺。例如，一家公司有各种不同的投资人，实现回报的时间点也大不相同。公司试图维护与每个投资人的关系，但所做的都是公司认为能够促进长期价值的事情。一家保险公司的首席执行官主张公司要高度公开。他对待股东就像对待共同拥有公司的手足兄弟，和他们讨论自己担心的问题、各种业务的价值、这些业务的竞争优势有多持久，以及计划如何分配资金等。他说："首席执行官绝对把一切归功于股东。我坚信，每位投资人都有权获得同样的信息，包括公司的估值前景和人员信息，正如一位沉默的合伙人所应该知道的一样。"

是否发布盈利指南预期是上市公司与投资人打交道时面临的最棘手问题之一。我们建议：若无必要，则不发布；若发布，则需给自己留足余地。

2. 中译英

China keeps optimizing the market environment and policies for Internet businesses, and a number of such businesses with innovation vitality and development potential have been cultivated, with their international competitiveness increased. By December 2021, there were 155 Chinese Internet businesses that had gone public at home or abroad, with a growth of 5.4 percent in comparison of that in 2020. There were 219 unicorn Internet businesses, and such businesses with the scale of over one hundred million *yuan* keep emerging. They are brilliant stars promoting the development of digital economy. Cross-border e-commerce is a strategy for the internationalization of China's e-commerce retail. Rapid development of digital economy is contributing to the country's broader integration into the global economic development.

第五单元

1. 英译中

神奇的滑雪区、完美的平整滑道、覆盖着厚厚积雪的绝佳雪坡——瑞士可以满足滑雪者的所有梦想。对于滑雪爱好者而言，位于滑雪区中心地带的酒店更是锦上添花：可滑雪进出的酒店意味着醒来一起床就能前往滑雪山坡。

可滑雪进出的酒店位于滑雪场的高处，为游客准备了在雪地上度过难忘假期所需的一切。独特的美食和瑞士热情好客的传统一定会让入住这些酒店的游客感到宾至如归。

积雪山坡上的一天无论多么精彩，总有结束之时。不过，在可滑雪进出的酒店，这都不是问题，从运动模式转换为派对模式最简单不过了。无论滑雪后在酒吧或舞池停留多久，您都很清楚明天早上一起床就能出去滑雪。

2. 中译英

Xi'an City Wall and Beilin Museum are world-famous historical and cultural attractions. The former, made up of the ancient city wall, the moat, the round-the-city woods, and the Shuncheng Road, is the most complete fortification complex that has survived in China. The Beilin Museum is a Chinese cultural art treasure, with the earliest and most famous steles from ancient China. Ascending the City Wall at the South Gate and walking all the way east from the South Gate, you can see the Beilin Museum at the end; standing at the entrance of the Museum, you can look up and see the magnificent City Wall. Adjacent to each other, the two form a must-see for tourists.

第六单元

1. 英译中

使用数字符号的传统计算正达到极限。不可否认，计算能力呈历史性指数级增长，大大改善了人类的条件。但是，这种增长已成为历史，其中很大一部分原因是受物理以及当下各种系统结构的限制。硬件设备的设计者努力消除纳米级热力波动产生的影响，而制作工厂成本激增使多家公司不再生产芯片。经济体系、生态系统、医药、社会系统、战争以及自动驾驶等复杂领域的软件开发者对有效计算的抽象及实现进行假设和编程的能力显然受到了挑战，包括深度神经网络在内的机器学习技术能够提供一定的帮助，但其能力有限。

2. 中译英

The direct effect of noise on human body is the harm to hearing. For instance, repeated exposure to noise or one long exposure to it may lead to nerve deafness. Besides its harm to ears and hearing, noise can affect our eyes and eyesight. According to findings of some experiments, the sensitivity of human's visual cells decreases in case of noise of 90 DB and it takes longer time to identify weak light in such a case; 40 percent of human beings have pupil dilation and blurred vision in case of noise of 95 DB; and most human beings' adaptation to light weakens in different degrees in case of noise of 115 DB. Therefore, those who are long exposed to noise are likely to suffer eyestrain, ophthalmalgia, blurred eyesight, and lachrymation.

第七单元

1. 英译中

如果经销商控制权在签订本协议日的任何时间被尚无经销商控制权的人或相关群体获得，经销商应立即向公司提供书面通知对这些人或群体予以说明，公司有权在收到经销商书面通知28日内向经销商发出书面通知两个月后终止本协议。

协议的终止不影响任何一方于协议终止前所拥有的权利或应承担的赔偿责任。

一方放弃追究另一方违反本协议某项规定的行为，不应被视为放弃追究以后的违约行为。

如本协议终止，公司可按照购买价格从经销商处回购经销商持有的存货。如经销商在协议终止之前已经获得了客户的订单，经销商也可销售这些产品。

2. 中译英

Article 26 The registered capital of a limited liability company shall be the amount of capital contributions subscribed for by all its shareholders as registered with the company registration authority. Where any law or administrative regulation or any decision of the State Council provides otherwise for the paid-in registered capital or the minimum amount of registered capital of a limited liability company, such provisions shall prevail.

Article 27 A shareholder may make capital contributions in cash, in kind, or intellectual property right, land-use right, or other non-monetary properties that may be assessed on the basis of currency and may be transferred according to the law, excluding the properties that shall not be treated as capital contributions under any law or administrative regulation. The value of the non-monetary properties as capital contributions shall be assessed and verified, which shall not be over-valued or under-valued. If any law or administrative regulation provides for the value assessment, such law or administrative regulation shall be followed.

Article 28 Each shareholder shall make full payment for the capital contributions he has subscribed to according to the bylaw. If a shareholder makes his capital contributions in cash, he shall deposit the full amount of such cash capital contributions into a temporary bank account opened for the limited liability company. If any capital contributions are made in non-monetary properties, the appropriate transfer procedures for the property rights therein shall be followed according to law. Where a shareholder fails to make his capital contributions as specified in the preceding paragraph, he shall not only make full payment to the company but also bear the liabilities for breach of contract to the shareholders who have made full payment of capital contributions on schedule.

第八单元

1. 英译中

尊敬的李先生：

您好！

我方于上月从贵方订购了24台Tanson 1 GHz奔腾X型电脑。当时商谈发货日期时，贵方承诺12月2日前发货，但如今距离商定发货的最后日期已过去两周时间，我方尚未收到贵方来函确认最终发货日期。

我方迫切需要这批电脑来优化行政办公能力，贵方延迟发货已给我方造成很大不便。

烦请过问此事，并请于三日内安排发货。如贵方无法在此期限内发货，恐怕我方将不得不取消订单，向其他供货方订货。

此致

敬礼！

行政办公室经理

卡迪尔·艾博

2020年12月16日

2. 中译英

July 20, 2020

Dear Mr. Parker,

We are concluding our visit to B&G Company and leaving for Beijing.

As we are departing, I would like to extend, on behalf of my company, our heartfelt gratitude for your hospitality. We all believe that our visit is a successful one, which will contribute to our further cooperation.

It is our sincere hope that you will visit us in Beijing, so that we will have an opportunity to repay your hospitality. Both my colleagues and I will be pleased to hold a banquet in your and your colleagues' honor. Then we can have a discussion on our closer and broader cooperation.

All the best wishes to you.

Wang Li

Sales Manager

×× Co. Ltd.

第九单元

1. 英译中

根据《消除对妇女一切形式歧视公约》和《北京行动纲要》的规定，我们已经取得了进展，特别是在以下领域：

- 推进法律改革。该措施旨在消除歧视，进一步保障妇女在法律各个领域的权利，特别是《家庭法》和《劳动法》中的权利。法律改革使得国家法律与相关的国际文书统一起来。
- 促进妇女经济独立。通过各种措施加强工作与家庭责任之间的协调，提倡同工同酬和保护产妇，改善职业指导和培训，并支持妇女创业计划。
- 通过培训计划实现政治领域中男女人数平衡。培训计划旨在鼓励和支持妇女参政，为政党中的妇女创造更有利的环境。

2. 中译英

We should adhere to multilateral and multiparty participation in the international cyberspace governance, and allow the government, international organizations, Internet businesses, technical communities, social organizations, and individual citizens to play their main roles. It is necessary to promote network governance within the UN framework and to give full play to the role of various non-state actors.

Interconnection is the basic nature of cyberspace and the fundamental guarantee for maintaining the vitality and continuous development of the Internet. Strengthening open cooperation in cyberspace is an important goal in building a community of shared future in cyberspace. It is necessary to promote bilateral, regional and international cooperation at different levels on an open basis, jointly build a platform for communication and cooperation, strengthen the complementarity of resource strengths, and achieve common development.

第十单元

1. 英译中

据印度尼西亚搜救机构消息，印度尼西亚巴厘岛周六上午发生4.8级地震，至少造成三人死亡。

该机构在一份声明中表示，地震影响这座观光岛东部的卡朗阿森和邦利地区。目前，搜救工作已经结束，不过相关部门仍在持续监测现场情况。

该机构称，地震引发的山体滑坡导致两人死亡，第三名遇难者被坠落的瓦砾击中而亡。

美国地质调查局（USGS）认为，此次4.8级地震发生在班贾尔地区附近，震源深度为10公里（约6.21英里）。

据当地媒体报道，尽管邻近的龙目岛也有震感，但地震并没有给巴厘岛其他地区造成重大损失。

巴厘岛因疫情限制国际游客入境18个月之后，于周四重新开放，但预计本月晚些时候，国际游客才会开始抵达巴厘岛。

2. 中译英

From October 18 to 26, the large-scale Beijing Opera orchestral suite “Grand Canal of Beijing City” toured in seven cities: Shanghai, Hangzhou, Nanjing, Yangzhou, Nantong, Ningbo, and Suzhou. This “Beijing Grand Opera” is produced by Beijing Municipal Bureau of Culture and Tourism, jointly played by Beijing Symphony Orchestra, Jingju Theater Company of Beijing and Beijing Musicians Association Chorus, and funded by Beijing Culture and Arts Fund.

“Grand Canal of Beijing City” is China’s first theatrical work based on the Grand Canal of Beijing. It is an integration of traditional Beijing Opera and Western symphony music, depicting the development of the Beijing section of the Grand Canal and highlighting the unique historical and cultural landscape of the city. The work includes an overture and four movements: "Seeing Tongzhou through the Tower Shadow", "Guo Shoujing, the Star in the Sky", "The Floating Beijing City", and "Tribute to the Grand Canal", which are presented with a variety of stage elements such as integrated choreography, lighting, costumes, and multimedia. It is an ambitious and epic performance.

主要参考文献

Bargiela-Chiappini, F. & Nickerson, C. *Writing Business: Genres, Media and Discourse*. London: Routledge, 1999.

De Waard, J. & Nida, E. A. *From One Language to Another: Functional Equivalence in Bible Translating*. Nashville: Thomas Nelson Publishers, 1986.

Ellis, M. & Johnson, C. *Teaching Business English*. Shanghai: Shanghai Foreign Language Education Press, 2002.

Hutchinson, T. & Waters, A. *English for Specific Purposes*. Cambridge: Cambridge University Press, 1987.

Newmark, P. *A Textbook of Translation*. Shanghai: Shanghai Foreign Language Education Press, 2001.

Nord, C. *Translating as a Purposeful Activity: Functionalist Approaches Explained*. Shanghai: Shanghai Foreign Language Education Press, 2001.

Paltridge, B. & Starfield, S. *The Handbook of English for Specific Purposes*. Chichester: John Wiley & Sons, Inc., 2013.

Reiss, K. *Translation Criticism: The Potentials & Limitations*. trans. Rhodes, E. F. Shanghai: Shanghai Foreign Language Education Press, 2004.

傅勇林，唐跃勤. 科技翻译. 北京：外语教学与研究出版社，2012.

顾维勇. 实用文体翻译. 北京：国防工业出版社，2005.

康志洪. 科技翻译. 北京：外语教学与研究出版社，2011.

李定坤. 汉英辞格对比与翻译. 武汉：华中师范大学出版社，1994.

李明. 商务英语翻译（汉译英）. 北京：高等教育出版社，2007.

李克兴. 法律翻译理论与实践. 北京：北京大学出版社，2007.

刘其中. 新闻翻译教程. 北京：中国人民大学出版社，2004.

彭萍. 新编商务英语翻译教程. 北京：商务印书馆，2021.

彭萍. 旅游英语综合教程. 北京：对外经济贸易大学出版社，2021.

彭萍. 英汉笔译. 北京：外语教学与研究出版社，2017.

彭萍. 实用商务翻译（英汉双向）. 北京：中国宇航出版社，2015.

彭萍. 实用旅游英语翻译（英汉双向）（第二版）. 北京：对外经济贸易大学出版社，2016.

彭萍. 实用英汉对比与翻译（英汉双向）. 北京：中译出版社，2015.

盛楠. 实用科技英语教程（第三版）. 北京：人民邮电出版社，2012.

张法连. 法律英语翻译教程. 北京：北京大学出版社，2016.